Raising Emotional Intelligence In Kids

How to Give Your Kids the Best Kickstart to Conquer Life

Sienna Neel

Contents

My Top 7 Essential Games to Boost Communication Skills In Children

(Make Learning Fun With These Perfect Tools!)

Checklist Includes:

- 7 Essential Games to Aid Child Development.
- Improve Family Bonding
- Encourages creativity and boost's self confidence
- Links to where you an buy these games for lowest prices.

If your're looking for hacks to accelerate your childs development then this is for you ....

Visit the Link Or Scan the QR Code to get this FREE Bonus Checklist

https://tinyurl.com/Sienna-Checklist

Introduction

"Our emotions need to be as educated as our intellect. It is important to know how to feel, how to respond and how to let life in so that it can touch you."—Anonymous

E motional intelligence is perhaps the most reliable measure of how successful someone will be in life. According to studies, a person's level of emotional intelligence accounts for almost 60% of their ability to succeed in their relationships and career regardless of the field they work in, and 90% of top performers are highly emotionally intelligent (Trotta, 2018, para. 10-11). While other factors like a good education and support from family and friends also play a role in determining one's future, the importance of emotional intelligence cannot be understated. Like many things in our lives, the seeds of emotional intelligence are planted during our childhoods.

We all have emotions, but we don't always know how to name or deal with them. This is especially true for young kids, who may not yet have the vocabulary or emotional maturity to identify how they feel. It's all too common for kids to burst into tears at the drop of a hat, throw an angry tantrum when something doesn't go their way, or respond to a new situation with fear instead of curiosity. Kids often have trouble explaining why they're upset, what caused them to feel this way, and what can be done to resolve the issue. This tends to manifest as kids who are 'difficult' and seem to be purposefully evasive or aggravating, even when they're really just confused.

It's tempting to get frustrated and assume your child is reacting this way because they're being fussy, or that they're purposefully trying to aggravate you. The truth is that your child just hasn't developed the skills to put what's wrong into words yet. If you can show them how to understand emotions and express them intelligently, they'll get a handle on these outbursts, and you'll have an easier time resolving whatever issue caused the distress in the first place.

Of course, emotional intelligence is important for everyone to know, not just kids. When you can assess how you're feeling and what made you feel this way, you can keep yourself calm in stressful situations, properly communicate the problem to others, and work toward a solution. When kids don't learn these skills in early childhood and instead continue to express or repress their emotions in unhealthy ways, they create a pattern of behavior that can follow them long into their adult years. However, if you teach your child emotional intelligence, you'll lay the groundwork for fewer tantrums when they're young and less explosive arguments as they get older. The better your child becomes at communicating how they feel, the better they'll be at listening and problem solving too.

Talking to your child about their emotions doesn't have to feel like interrogating an unwilling participant. Kids can learn to open up about their feelings and have a mature, honest discussion, but first, they need to understand how to name their feelings and effectively communicate them. Whether you're a parent, guardian, or educator, helping your child develop emotional intelligence skills will improve not only your relationship with them but also all of your child's current and future relationships.

If the idea of teaching emotional intelligence is new to you, don't worry; you can still learn and pass these skills onto your child, and incorporate them into your own interactions as well. In *Raising Emotional Intelligence in Kids*, you'll discover why emotional intelligence is so critical to good communication and what it means to be emotionally intelligent. You'll also learn how to help your child find their way through the often complex, confusing maze that is their emotions, assisting them in defining, explaining, and resolving their feelings in a healthy way. As your child learns how to talk about their feelings and understand the feelings of others, tantrums will become less common as more efficient communication methods become the norm instead. You'll have fewer fights, and your child will likely find it easier to make and keep friends. Emotional intelligence is a key factor in getting kids to listen, behave, and prepare themselves for the real world. Reading this book gives you all the tools you need to give this gift to your child.

As a personal life coach, philanthropist, and someone who has a long history of working with kids, it's clear to me just how important emotional intelligence is as a skill everyone should learn, starting in their younger years. I have a first-hand understanding of the difficulties that come from kids who haven't yet developed emotional intelligence, as well as the benefits that come from improving your child's understanding of emotions. I have been studying child behavioral psychology for over 10 years, and during this time I've seen that kids who are encouraged to develop emotional maturity early on in their lives greatly improve their chances of being successful, well-adjusted adults. This book is a way to help as many parents as possible to raise their kids in a way that builds and supports healthy child development by meeting their social needs.

Good communication is one of the most important foundational skills every child should know to help them socialize with their parents, guardians, and peers. This is just as true for the contents of this book as it is in my previous parenting book, *SHHHH...Listen!: Practical Parenting Steps to Get Your Kids to Listen That Work! Age 3-8*. In this book, I focused primarily on how to improve listening and communication with your child through a better understanding of child psychology and anger management for both parent and child. Emotional intelligence involves using healthy communication strategies as well. Through assisting your child in understanding and better managing their emotions, you can improve your relationship with your child and reach a deeper level of understanding with each other.

If you're sick of fights, tantrums, and unexplained fits of crying, teaching your child emotional intelligence can be your ticket to a less complicated relationship with them. This also paves the way for your child's future success later in life, as those who are emotionally attuned develop the charisma they need to excel both professionally and socially. By improving your child's emotional awareness and expression, not only are you giving them an invaluable skill, you're also solidifying your bond with them for years to come.

Chapter 1

Unlocking the Power of Emotional Intelligence

D espite the clear importance of emotional intelligence during every stage of our lives, it's not an especially well-known term. Our society tends to focus, and therefore prioritize, more traditional methods of measuring intelligence. Kids are asked to memorize information, and they're then graded on how well they retain this information on different tests and quizzes. As adults, intelligence becomes a badge of honor, and we tend to associate successful people with a high intellect. For all the time we spend holding up this view of intelligence that is measured by our cognitive abilities, the value of emotional intelligence tends to fall by the wayside, despite its importance.

Emotional intelligence has less to do with memorizing and recalling various facts. Like cognitive intelligence, it requires critical thinking and problem-solving skills, but these skills are applied to work out the solutions to emotional problems rather than, for example, mathematical ones. Emotional intelligence is a way of measuring someone's ability to express their emotions clearly and appropriately, to understand others' emotions through their behaviors and words, and to associate different triggers and outcomes with certain emotions. Someone who is highly emotionally intelligent can figure out what emotion they're feeling and why they might be feeling that way and then take steps to correct unwanted or excessive emotions without either shutting themselves off or overreacting. They can also pick up on cues from other people that indicate how they might be feeling, and adjust their own behaviors to account for this. An emotionally intelligent person typically has a good idea of how people react when they experience different emotions, and they can use this to predict and accommodate the reactions of others. Emotionally intelligent people tend to be charismatic, compassionate, and understanding, which is part of the reason why they are well-liked and often find success.

Emotional intelligence can also be seen as a measure of how well we can communicate with other people, both in our ability to understand their wants and needs, and to discern and share our own. If we can improve our emotional intelligence, we can avoid many fights and misunderstandings that might otherwise harm our relationships. By being in tune with our feelings, we can more easily navigate the world around us and interact with family, friends, and strangers alike.

Developing emotional intelligence is especially important for kids. When kids are young, they form their first social connections within the family, with educators, and with their peers. A lack of control over their emotions, and an inability to understand their peers' emotions, could harm these early relationships. For example, if your child gets frustrated and throws a tantrum instead of trying to communicate why they're upset, a teacher might start thinking of them as unruly and spend less time trying to connect with them in the classroom. This might also drive their fellow students away, especially if there is aggression involved. If your child doesn't understand social cues that indicate their friend is upset, they might not realize it until they're crying. They may not know how to apologize for pushing too hard and crossing a boundary, which could strain their friendships. On the other hand, if your child learns more about their emotions and the emotions of others, they can connect with their peers and create positive social connections.

"Punishment is the Best Way to Discipline"

Many parents believe that strict punishment is necessary to teach children discipline. However, this approach often leads to negative self-esteem and does not address the underlying emotional needs of the child.

While childhood is an especially important stage in developing emotional intelligence, this pursuit shouldn't end there. Becoming more emotionally attuned should be a lifelong goal. Emotional intelligence is just as important for maintaining relationships and good mental health as an adult as it is for a child. As you guide your child through a basic understanding of emotions and the effects they can have on people, you provide them with the foundations of emotional intelligence, which they will ideally continue to build on for the rest of their lives.

Five Basic Parts of Emotional Intelligence

There are five core components of emotional intelligence. These are self-awareness, self-regulation, motivation, empathy, and social skills (Ohio University, n.d., para. 2-6). Each one represents a different aspect of social relationships or personal assessment, and each of them are important to learn for different situations.

Self-Awareness

It's very common for kids to lack the vocabulary to explain how they're feeling. For young kids, this means learning what basic emotions such as 'sad,' 'angry,' 'excited,' and 'nervous' mean, and what they feel like. Older kids may need an introduction to more complex feelings like 'jealousy,' 'grief,' and 'insecurity.' A child who is self-aware in regard to their feelings should be able to identify and tell you what emotion they're experiencing. They'll also start to understand how their feelings impact others. For example, they might see how when they get mad and start yelling and making a scene, you become frustrated with them or upset in turn.

Help your child identify their emotions so they get the hang of doing it themselves. Teach them what different emotions feel like so they'll know how to describe them when they encounter them. Let's say you ask your child to put their toys away and they begin to cry because they want to keep playing. Ask them how they're feeling—are they sad because they want to keep playing, or angry or worried because of what you're asking them to do instead? You can also share with them how that makes you feel, as their parent or guardian. For example, you might be sad and frustrated when they don't listen to you. From here, you can have more in-depth discussions about why they feel this way and what can be done to soothe them.

Self-Regulation

Many kids throw tantrums when things aren't going their way. They work themselves up until they are irreconcilably upset or completely furious, and they need to expend that energy—often in inappropriate, aggressive ways—before they feel calm again. This isn't a healthy method for managing emotions, and it can develop into more harmful coping mechanisms as these kids grow older.

Kids who are able to self-regulate are more in control of how they display their feelings. While emotions should never be suppressed, there are constructive and destructive ways to express them, and relying on destructive methods too often can make it harder for them to get a handle on their feelings. Self-regulation involves your child recognizing how they feel, controlling how they choose to express that feeling, and understanding the consequences of whatever form of expression they choose. A child who throws tantrums might put more stress on their family or hurt their friends' feelings. They may also receive a time-out or other punishment for inappropriate behaviors. These are important consequences for kids to learn and consider so they can choose to act accordingly. Instead of throwing a tantrum, a child may pause, recognize they might get in trouble and that the tantrum won't get them what they want, and talk about their feelings clearly instead.

Motivation

Emotions can have a significant impact on motivation. If your child is distracted, upset, frustrated, or anxious, they may have more difficulty getting their work done than they would if they were in a happier mood. It's easy to be motivated when there is very little emotional resistance, but it can be much harder if these feelings interfere with their usual motivation levels.

Kids with a good grasp on emotional intelligence typically find it easier to get important work done regardless of these distracting negative feelings. They should be able to complete classwork as instructed and to do chores around the house. For example, if they don't get the snack they wanted with their lunch, more motivated kids will be able to return to their classroom and focus on the next task the teacher assigns them without feeling distracted by their sadness or frustration. It is normal for kids to take breaks and "recharge their batteries" if they're going through a difficult experience, but they must also learn to compartmentalize these emotions from time to time so they don't fall behind on their responsibilities.

Note that not every issue with motivation can be traced back to regular difficulties understanding and processing emotions. Sometimes this may be connected to more serious mental health issues or difficulties in your child's life, or it may be the result of an attention deficit disorder. If you believe your child's lack of motivation may come from one of these sources, speak with a pediatrician about possible diagnosis and treatment options.

Empathy

Empathy is your child's ability to understand how someone else feels and relate it back to their own feelings. Most kids do not develop empathy until they are around two years old, after which point they should begin to pay more attention to the emotions of others. This can be a difficult skill to develop and practice even for some adults, but far from impossible, especially if empathy is encouraged at a young age.

Empathy allows your child to adjust their behaviors to respond to the feelings of others. They can show compassion because they understand what someone else is going through. As an example, let's say your child is playing a game with one of their friends. Their friend is losing the game, and they're visibly frustrated. A child who hasn't yet built up their empathy skills might continue beating them without regard for how they're feeling, or worse, tease them for losing. On the other hand, an empathetic child may allow their friend to win, or try to find another compromise that doesn't lead to tears. By seeing how their friend feels and adjusting their behavior accordingly, your child uses empathy to maintain social relationships.

Social Skills

Social skills are both a component and an important result of developing emotional intelligence. It is hard for kids to create and maintain friendships if they fail to understand others' emotions and regulate their own. As they practice their social skills, managing relationships with peers and authority figures in their lives, they'll strengthen their social connections, which is very important to healthy cognitive development.

Working with others, practicing patience, and having good manners are key social skills for every child to learn. These are foundational requirements for most healthy relationships. Kids who are socially capable often excel in the classroom and have more positive home lives as well, since they are able to listen, communicate, and understand the actions of others. These kids have the social skills needed to see a rowdy child and offer them a toy to play with as a distraction or to approach a lonely child during recess and invite them into their game. They use their socialization skills to forge bonds with others and often make life-long friends as a result.

Each of the five aspects of emotional intelligence is key to socialization and communication. Throughout the rest of the book, we'll go into more detail about how you can teach your child mastery over these skills through various games and conversations.

Cognitive Versus Emotional Intelligence

Cognitive intelligence has traditionally been much higher valued than its emotional equivalent. The modern education system focuses heavily on increasing kids' cognitive capabilities, and it spends very little time helping them develop emotional intelligence skills, primarily because cognitive intelligence is usually seen as the greatest predictor of future success. But how true is this assumption? To find out, we must first examine both kinds of intelligence and their outcomes on child development.

Cognitive intelligence is measured by a child's intelligence quotient (IQ). Usually, IQ is determined through a standardized test. It's a single number that reflects how cognitively capable someone is, testing their mental and academic abilities. Some of the skills tested include reasoning, memory, comprehension, processing speed, and more. Kids may be asked to complete questions about pattern recognition, logical reasoning, visual and spatial awareness, arithmetic, and making analogies, similar to the skills they learn in standard classroom education.

While these skills are certainly important and necessary for many jobs, are they really an accurate representation of a child's capabilities as they've come to be known? IQ tests often split kids into 'average,' 'above average,' and 'below average' categories, and this categorization can discourage kids from putting enough effort into their studies to improve their IQ. On top of this, IQ may not be as important in our daily lives as we're led to believe. Its accuracy in predicting future success is mixed at best. In short, if you're looking for a single standardized test number to determine if your child will have a good life, you're probably not going to find it through the IQ test.

Now, let's consider a more emotional approach to intelligence. The measurement of emotional intelligence is known as the emotional quotient (EQ). This represents a child's social-emotional skills as understood through their ability to be self-aware, self-regulatory, motivated, empathetic, and social. Standardized tests for measuring EQ are less common. Instead, it is more readily understood by observing kids' behaviors and paying attention to how they interact with others.

A child's EQ, though it isn't always treated with the same seriousness as IQ, may be very important for their development. Socialization is critical during our formative years, and poor emotional intelligence can lead to equally poor social skills. Improving kids' EQs, not just their IQs, shows promise as a way to better prepare our kids for navigating the complexities of the adult world.

	IQ	EQ
Abilities	Heightened cognitive abilities, reasoning skills, logical capabilities, memory, comprehension, and processing speed	Motivation, good social skills, awareness of others' feelings, awareness of their own feelings, and control over their own emotions
Qualities	Academic curiosity, low impulsivity, frequently disorganized, and sometimes lacking a large social circle	Compassion and empathy, good work-life balance, charisma, and frequent emotional expression
Identifiers	Good grades in school, rapid understanding of more difficult concepts, good reading and math comprehension, and seeking out knowledge without being prompted	A large or close friend group, good behavior with few outbursts, willingness to help others, self-confidence, and friendliness toward others

Which Is More Important?

Both IQ and EQ may play a role in how successful your child grows up to be. That being said, the role they play may not be equal. Traditional thought would have us give the edge to cognitive intelligence, but some modern psychologists have started suggesting that emotional intelligence plays a far greater role.

One prominent advocate of EQ's superiority is psychologist and author Daniel Goleman. He believes that "emotional intelligence predicts future success in relationships, health and quality of life" (Kadane, 2020, para. 5) far more accurately than a child's IQ score. High EQ is believed to lead to impressive outcomes such as healthier choices, greater motivation and mental clarity, less risk of getting involved in bullying, and easier adaptation when working as part of a team.

Of course, kids still need to develop their cognitive skills. But in this, too, EQ can often be an asset. Kids who have high emotional intelligence often excel and school, with their cognitive intelligence improving as a result of their abstract thinking, reasoning, and language skills. They have an easier time labeling and discussing their emotions with others, and they can work through emotional roadblocks that might interfere with motivation for other kids. They may also find it easier to ask for help when they don't understand a task, which can make a huge difference in how long they struggle with a new skill before mastering it.

While both IQ and EQ are important, emotional intelligence seems to have a greater impact on who your child will grow up to become. The benefits of emotional intelligence are many, and they are worth cultivating in every child to give them the best life possible.

Benefits of Emotional Intelligence

As already mentioned, emotional intelligence can impact kids in a number of different ways. On top of more obvious improvements in cognitive abilities, managing the expression of negative emotions, relationship management, and future career success, kids with high EQs also generally have fewer mental health issues thanks to their abilities to understand and talk about their feelings. EQ may even have an impact on the immune system, yielding an improved resistance to illness. These benefits are just those that have been studied as of now; it is possible that with more time and research, a whole host of other advantages will be discovered, and this will become just the tip of the emotional intelligence iceberg.

The Connection Between IQ and EQ

IQ and EQ may seem to be polar opposites at first, but they're actually far more connected than you might think. As previously mentioned, emotional intelligence can assist kids in improving their cognitive abilities, whether in the classroom or in applying these skills to real-world problems. They frequently do better on standardized exams, and their logical reasoning and critical thinking skills often improve as well. There are a number of reasons for this. It may be a product of a willingness to look for more inventive solutions to different problems. The ability to take an empathetic, compassionate approach to an issue and see things from someone else's point of view is ideal for problem-solving. Kids with high EQs also tend to be more motivated and focused when completing their schoolwork, without the burden of being distracted by unresolved emotions. They can better absorb what's in front of them, and they're often more excited to go to school so they can see their friends. Whatever the reason, if you want to assist your child in improving their cognitive skills, you might be better off starting with emotional skills first.

Healthy Relationships

Emotional intelligence is a key factor in efficient communication, which goes hand in hand with healthy relationships. Since kids with high EQs can identify what others are feeling, and they can get a handle on their own feelings without shouting or hitting, they're often excellent at conflict resolution. There may also be fewer fights in general, as these kids are mature enough to talk about something that hurt their feelings rather than suppressing the hurt until they have an outburst. High EQ kids often develop deeper friendships as well, as they broach more serious topics with their friends and have a genuine understanding of each other. They are likely to have few problems talking to new people and maintaining a friend group throughout their early childhoods, and these skills will benefit them later in life when they start pursuing romantic relationships.

Adulthood Success

The early years of kids' lives lay the groundwork for their teenage and adult years. Achieving success as an adult isn't entirely dependent on having a healthy childhood, but this certainly helps kids get a head start. One study published in the *American Journal of Public Health* tracked a group of kids' development for 19 years. The study found that "a child's social and emotional skills in kindergarten may predict lifelong success. Children who were able to share, cooperate, and follow directions at age five were more likely to obtain college degrees and to begin working full-time jobs by age 25" (Morin, 2019, para. 6). As parents and guardians, we always want our kids to be successful and grow up to achieve only the best things in life. Giving them a good foundation of emotional intelligence provides them with the tools they need to excel in life.

Mental Health

Mental health problems like anxiety, depression, and bipolar disorder are closely tied to emotions. Kids who are highly emotionally intelligent may be better able to navigate these emotions and be less at risk for suffering from mental health issues. Those who do experience a mood disorder such as depression at some point in their lives often seek treatment earlier and find more success with it, as they have less difficulty speaking honestly about their emotions. Emotional intelligence does not always prevent these conditions from occurring, but it may make them less likely.

Self-Soothing

When some kids get upset, they continue to work themselves up and make the problem worse. What starts as a small scare from a scraped knee or a brief sadness caused by something their friend said rapidly evolves into a full-on meltdown that catches the attention of everyone in the area. However, emotionally intelligent kids don't typically follow this path. A child who understands their feelings is better able to come to terms with them and calm themselves down before the situation can escalate. This saves you a headache as a parent, and it also benefits your child in the long run. Self-soothing as a child makes it easier to remain calm as an adult, and it may reduce the risk of developing aggression issues and severe phobias as an adult.

Resistance to Physical Illness

While most of the results of emotional intelligence are seen in a child's thoughts and actions, it's possible it can have a physical impact as well. When we're stressed, our immune system weakens. We have a harder time fighting off illness, leaving us vulnerable to colds and other viruses. Emotionally intelligent kids are better at stress management, so their immune systems are able to function properly. Therefore, kids with high EQs may fall ill less frequently than their peers.

The Importance of Developing Emotional Intelligence During Early Childhood

Early childhood is a very volatile period with a lot of change. It's the point at which kids learn language, social interaction, and an ever-expanding understanding of the world around them. Emotional intelligence is just as important for kids to learn during this time. Most kids undergo the majority of their cognitive development during their younger years, as they start to interact with more people on a more frequent basis.

Prior to attending classes, your child's social circle is probably limited to family and a few close friends, or perhaps some neighbors. The vast majority of social interaction a child experiences during these years comes from their immediate family. As kids start to grow up and attend school, they'll meet and begin to bond with their teachers, their fellow students, and other people outside of the family. Each new conversation carries an emotional message, representing a new experience in your child's life that they can learn from. The more conversations they have and social connections they form, the more these messages repeat, eventually forming the very core of your child's emotional abilities and their outlook. If you encourage your child to be more emotionally aware, they'll solidify a positive relationship with their emotions that they'll carry with them for years to come. The earlier kids learn to understand their feelings and the feelings of others, the easier it will be for them to practice these key skills for the rest of their lives.

The Beginnings of Self-Evaluation

Early childhood is also the point at which kids begin to turn their attention inward and evaluate themselves. They begin to make judgments about who they are and what they're capable of. This can be influenced by our expectations of them and how we react when they do something we don't like.

Prior to engaging in self-evaluation, kids form their ideas of themselves based on what the authority figures in their lives say. If they clean up around the house and you tell them they're being very helpful, this contributes to a positive self-image. If they make a mistake on a homework assignment and you tell them they're not good at math, they'll begin to believe this about themselves too, even if they haven't been given the time to improve. Later on, when kids start evaluating themselves, they might develop a positive or negative self-image based on how you guide their development.

According to the child psychologist Erik Erikson, this period of early self-evaluation is known as "autonomy versus shame and doubt." Kids may view themselves as either an autonomous person capable of growth and achievement or their vision may be clouded by guilt and shame, inhibiting a positive view of themselves. As Erikson claims,

"Young children who feel autonomous see themselves as good, valuable people who are able to do what is expected of them in a positive way. In contrast, young children who feel ashamed also feel worthless and incapable of doing what is expected of them" (Oswalt, n.d., para. 6). These feelings of doubt can be difficult to overcome as kids get older, so it's important to teach kids emotional intelligence and encourage them to view themselves in a positive light while their minds are still at their most receptive.

"Emotional Intelligence Can't Be Taught"

The misconception that emotional intelligence is an innate trait rather than a skill that can be developed leads to missed opportunities in nurturing these skills in children.

Rapid Cognitive Development During Childhood

We learn information at different rates throughout our lives. When we are young, we pick up our native language just by being exposed to it frequently, and it's easy to master a second language when our minds are still malleable. If you've ever tried to learn a foreign language as an adult, you know it's much harder. Our brains undergo more cognitive development and growth during the first three or four years of our lives than they will ever again. During this time, our brains grow to about two-thirds of their full size, and the pathways inside our brain rapidly evolve in complexity. This makes it easy to learn and internalize new information, especially in regard to emotional intelligence.

With so much development going on in such a short period of time, there is plenty for kids to learn. They are always noticing, thinking, processing, reacting, and adapting to their environments and the people around them. Their emotional experiences contribute to the ideas they hold about themselves, others, and the world at large, and these ideas become more difficult to change the longer they are held. Early childhood is the best time to instill emotional intelligence in kids to give them the best chance at success later in their lives.

Chapter 2

Becoming an Emotion Coach to Guide Your Child's Growth

A s a parent, teacher, or other guardian, you have the opportunity to have a profound impact on your child's emotional development. Depending on your actions, you might leave them to struggle with unknown feelings and allow them to express these emotions explosively, or you might guide them toward a healthy relationship with their inner selves. You are the emotion coach for your child. Whatever you teach them will stick with them and affect how they choose to carry themselves long after they've started a family with kids of their own.

Just like kids start to learn how to speak from listening to their parents, so too do they learn emotional intelligence first through observation.

Kids are remarkably perceptive, especially when they are young, despite how we tend to think things will go over their heads. Moments from their early childhoods can have a surprisingly significant impact, even if kids can't actually remember these moments when they grow up and their early childhood memories fade. It is incredibly important to start by cultivating emotional awareness in yourself as you begin teaching it to your child.

How Your Emotional Awareness Affects Childhood Development

In my previous book, *SHHHH...Listen!,* we took a look at how our own troubles with frustration and anger can rub off on our kids, subtly encouraging them to react the same way. If we get frustrated and resort to yelling when we don't get our way, our kids will see this, assume it's typical to behave this way, and become more prone to aggressive outbursts themselves. If we take a moment to gather ourselves when we're angry, and we don't take our anger out on our kids, they will learn to replicate this kind of behavior instead.

The same idea applies to all forms of emotional awareness. Kids learn by watching authority figures. They pick up the healthy and unhealthy coping mechanism we use. Let's say your child is being difficult while getting dressed in the morning. You might start yelling and forcing them into their clothes, fed-up with their behavior, but this only results in your child acting similarly aggressive when someone on the playground won't share with them. If we shove our emotions away, allow ourselves to get swept up in our feelings rather than regaining control over ourselves, and ignore how our kids feel in favor of imposing our own will upon them, they'll learn to do the same. If we look for an unhealthy way to keep ourselves calm like excessive drinking or smoking, they may see these vices as viable coping mechanisms as well. By acting as a good role model for our kids, we can show them what emotions look like, how to handle them, and how to respect others' feelings.

Assessing Your Own Emotional Intelligence

In order to teach a lesson, we must first understand it ourselves. This means taking an honest look at how we deal with issues and out-of-control emotions, especially in front of our kids.

Think about how you react when your child does something frustrating. Are you quick to anger? Do you raise your voice? Do you sometimes say things you don't really mean in the heat of the moment, not realizing what kind of impact it might have on your child? Or do you take a moment to calm yourself before reacting? Do you consider what might have driven your child to bad behavior, and how they might be feeling now? Can you keep a level head while still clearly communicating why what they did was wrong? These are important questions, as they reveal a great deal about your parenting approach and how you view emotions.

You might also have difficulty being empathetic when your child is upset, especially when the reason seems trivial. Have you ever told your child to "suck it up" when they were on the verge of tears, or told them not to be sad when something went wrong? While it's natural to want to see your child smiling and happy, it's also natural for everyone to express their emotions, and forcing away tears just to put on a happy face rarely helps kids calm themselves down. You might occasionally find yourself being dismissive of your child's wants and fears, which can subconsciously encourage them to disregard and shove down their feelings. To help your child deal with their emotions in the healthiest possible way, it's important to watch out for moments when your gut instinct is to dismiss your child's feelings. If they're upset because the weather is too cold to play outside, don't roll your eyes and ignore their distress. Instead, understand that this matters to your child and let them know when it will be warm enough again, or help them find fun indoor activities to do in the meantime. By altering your responses and becoming more receptive to seeing things from your child's point of view, you guide them toward a healthy expression of their emotions and greater emotional intelligence.

"Kids Will Naturally Outgrow Bad Behaviors Without Guidance"

Relying on children to outgrow bad behaviors without guidance can leave them without essential emotional skills. Active teaching helps them manage emotions, communicate effectively, and build stronger relationships.

Four Types of Parental Responses

When your child expresses emotional distress, there are a number of different ways you could respond. You might lend a sympathetic ear, try to find a solution for the problem, become upset yourself, or simply roll your eyes and wait for whatever's bothering them to pass. According to clinical psychologists John and Julie Gottman, who believe strongly in the importance of discovering the emotional source of behavioral issues, there are four possible routes for a parent to take when reacting to their kids' emotions. These parenting styles are the dismissing parent, the disapproving parent, the laissez-faire parent, and the emotion coach (Lisitsa, 2012, para. 3-6). Each parental archetype influences childhood development in a different way.

The Dismissing Parent

If you're a dismissing parent, you might find yourself retreating from emotional honesty. You may be used to ignoring and suppressing your own emotions, and as a result, you unknowingly encourage your child to do the same. It's possible you might catch yourself failing to take your child's emotions seriously, and when something upsets them, you may distract or chide them rather than helping them work through the feeling. These methods usually assume that with enough time, all pains fade, often neglecting to acknowledge that failing to properly address difficult moments leaves them unresolved.

> **Tim:** "Mom, I'm sad because I wasn't invited to Jake's birthday party."
>
> **Dismissing Parent:** "Oh, don't worry about it. These things happen all the time. It's not a big deal. Why don't you just go play with your toys?"
>
> **Tim:** "But I really wanted to go."
>
> **Dismissing Parent:** "You're making a fuss over nothing, Tim. Just forget about it. There will be other parties."
>
> **Effect:** Tim learns to suppress his feelings, believing that expressing emotions isn't important or valid, and may start to feel that his emotions are insignificant.

The child of a dismissing parent will likely internalize the idea that emotions are something to be feared. They may take anger, tears, and even outward expressions of joy and shove them down inside of themselves, and they can have greater difficulties regulating their emotions when these built-up feelings become too much to contain. Your child may also see their feelings as unnatural and unwanted, which can interfere with their ability to learn proper coping strategies.

The Disapproving Parent

You can recognize your tendencies toward being a disapproving parent if you react to your child's emotions with a more critical response. Rather than just ignoring the problem, you may notice you tend to actively discourage the expression of emotion. This often involves negative judgments, ridicule, and an authoritative parenting style that makes use of strict rules or harsh punishments for bad behavior.

> **Tim:** "Dad, I'm sad because I wasn't invited to Jake's birthday party."
>
> **Disapproving Parent:** "You need to toughen up, Tim. It's just a birthday party. Getting upset over something so small is silly. You shouldn't let things like this bother you."
>
> **Tim:** "But everyone else was invited."
>
> **Disapproving Parent:** "Well, maybe you should try harder to fit in. Stop being so sensitive. Life's tough, and you need to get used to it."
>
> **Effect:** Tim might feel ashamed of his emotions and start to internalize that showing feelings is wrong or weak, potentially leading to self-esteem issues and difficulty expressing himself in the future.

The effects of this parenting style are fairly similar to those of the dismissing parent but to an even greater extent. Kids may have self-esteem issues, trouble getting their feelings under control, or issues expressing emotions at all.

The Laissez-Faire Parent

The laissez-faire parent model is based on the economic policy of the same name, which means to take a "hands-off approach." If you're a laissez-faire parent, you may be far too lenient with your rules, to the extent that you rarely correct your child's behavior at all. You might have trouble offering any sort of guidance for your child as they navigate their way through their feelings, which can make it harder for them to solve emotional problems or even identify what they're feeling.

Tim: "Mom, I'm sad because I wasn't invited to Jake's birthday party."

Laissez-Faire Parent: "Oh, that's unfortunate. Well, do whatever makes you feel better. If you want, you can skip school tomorrow."

Tim: "Can I play video games all day then?"

Laissez-Faire Parent: "Sure, if that helps you feel better. Just make sure you don't let it get you too down."

Effect: Tim may struggle to learn how to handle disappointment and manage his emotions effectively, potentially leading to issues with impulse control, lack of guidance in dealing with emotions, and difficulties understanding boundaries.

The kids of laissez-faire parents often have difficulty concentrating. They may be more rambunctious and less likely to follow rules of any kind. Since they have little experience being taught to regulate their emotions and recognize others' emotions, forming friendships becomes a difficult task.

The Emotion Coach

The final type of parent is the emotion coach, and it's the gold standard that all parents should strive for. It's more emotion-positive than the dismissing or disapproving parent, and it offers more guidance than the laissez-faire method. Emotion coaches help their kids work through their feelings rather than leaving them to manage on their own or willing these emotions away. They are present when interacting with their kids, active listeners, and understanding yet firm in their rules. As a result, kids typically develop a healthy relationship with their emotions.

> **Tim:** "Dad, I'm sad because I wasn't invited to Jake's birthday party."

Emotion Coach: "I'm sorry to hear that, Tim. It sounds like you're feeling left out, and that's a tough feeling. Can you tell me more about why you think you weren't invited?"

Tim: "Maybe Jake doesn't like me."

Emotion Coach: "It's hard to know for sure, but it's okay to feel sad and confused. Sometimes people make choices that hurt our feelings, and it's important to talk about them. Let's think about some other fun things we can do, and maybe we can plan a fun activity together."

Tim: "Maybe we can go to the park?"

Emotion Coach: "That sounds like a great idea. And remember, just because you weren't invited this time doesn't mean you won't be included next time. It's also a good opportunity to think about what kind of friend you want to be. How about we talk about ways to handle situations like this in the future?"

Effect: Tim feels validated and learns that it's okay to express emotions. He also starts developing strategies to cope with difficult feelings, building resilience and emotional intelligence, and gaining a better understanding of social dynamics.

The emotion coach parenting strategy is fairly rare compared to the others, but it's not an impossible feat if you understand the basics. With a little time and practice, any parent can become an emotion coach for their child, no matter which of the other parenting styles you were previously aligned with.

"Expressing Emotions Should Be Limited to Avoid Overreaction"

Suppressing children's emotional expression to prevent overreaction can increase stress and lead to bigger outbursts. Encouraging healthy expression helps them process feelings and develop better emotional management skills.

The Five Steps of Emotion Coaching

To learn how to be an emotion coach, you must start with the five basic steps. These steps are intended to help you alter your reactions when your child needs some coaching. They can help you pump the breaks if you find yourself veering into disapproving territory, or remind you to start a conversation with your child even when you'd be more inclined to follow the laissez-faire approach of ignoring the issue. In a sense, they represent a streamlined method for becoming more involved in your child's emotional development. Adopting these simple approaches can make a world of difference in how you impact their EQ.

Pay Attention to Your Child's Emotions

Think of what happens in the immediate moments before you get upset. You might become more withdrawn. You might curl your hands into fists and stick out your chest for a more aggressive response, or hunch your shoulders forward in a more submissive posture. Kids have plenty of these same tells, and they're often easier to spot than they are on most adults. There are usually many different signs that indicate a more severe reaction is coming, but it's easy to miss them in your child if you're not giving the situation your full attention.

Encourage yourself to be more sensitive to how your child feels before they have to "amp up" their display. Look for signs that indicate they might be getting upset or frustrated so you can intervene before they begin crying or yelling. Kids tend to have the loudest outbursts when they feel no one is paying attention to them. If you learn to look for and recognize the signs of distress early, your child won't have to escalate their reaction to get you to acknowledge their feelings.

Use Emotional Expression as an Opportunity to Teach

It can be hard to feel comfortable talking about emotions if it's not something you're used to. If you grew up being encouraged to ignore your feelings, you might look at your child's emotions as more of an inconvenience or burden than anything else. It helps to alter how you think about the situation so you can respond to it more effectively. Instead of dreading emotional displays, consider how discussions about emotions can help you feel closer to your child. Look for teachable moments whenever possible, and use emotions as opportunities to discuss difficult topics and guide your child's development. When you start actively seeking out these moments instead of avoiding them, you can deepen the connection between you and your child by serving as a guiding force during a time of turmoil for them.

Listen to and Validate Your Child's Feelings

Paying more attention to your child can reveal a wealth of information hiding just below the surface. If your child is trying to talk to you about their emotions, give them your full focus. Put down whatever else you're working on and look them in the eye whenever possible. Help them feel like you care and you want them to succeed. If your child is upset but they can't or won't tell you what's wrong, giving them more of your attention could help point you toward a solution as well.

Part of being a good listener is confirming you've heard what the other person has to say. Listen actively, giving both verbal and nonverbal cues to show your interest. This could be as simple as a nod of your head, or as involved as repeating information back to your child after they say it. This shows them you understand what they're experiencing, and that you're going to help them through it.

Assist Your Child in Labeling Their Emotions

Many young kids lack the vocabulary needed to describe their feelings. They may also have trouble figuring out why they react in a certain way. You can assist them in learning what their emotions are called and what they mean. For example, if your child starts crying, you might ask them if they're feeling sad, lonely, or angry. You may also need to help them reach the answer. Spend some time teaching your child about different emotions so they'll know what to expect when these feelings rear their heads.

Help Your Child Problem-Solve With Limits

While emotional expression is natural, you also need to set limits regarding what's acceptable behavior and what's not. It's okay for your child to feel angry, but it's not okay for them to express that anger by hitting you. They need to find appropriate ways to deal with their anger, such as speaking about it or counting to 10 in their heads.

You can assist your child in establishing coping methods for difficult emotions. Help them develop their problem-solving skills so they can look for a solution to their issue without working themselves up over it. Once they stop focusing on the problem and start looking for the solution, the need to yell or hit may fade as their attention is directed elsewhere. You should also help your child create goals and make plans for achieving those goals. This gives them something to work toward, and something to remember when their emotions threaten to overwhelm them.

Exercises for Emotion Coaching Practice

Emotion coaching exercises can be very helpful as tools for education. They help you see emotions as opportunities for learning and for bonding with your child. The more frequently you talk to your child about their emotions, even your own, the easier they will find it to understand their feelings and develop a sense of empathy toward others.

If your child is feeling frustrated, upset, and misunderstood, take a moment to talk through these emotions with them. Treat them with the same respect and understanding you'd like to be treated with, and resist the urge to sweep their concerns under the rug, even if the source of their frustration doesn't seem like such a big deal to you. Kids are more likely to get upset about small things because they have experienced much less over the course of their lives. To them, not getting the toy they wanted may very well feel like the end of the world, and telling them it doesn't matter rarely helps them process their feelings. Instead, ask them why they are so upset, and help them understand the source of their problem.

It's also important to pay attention to how your child responds to your methods. If they seem to withdraw and go quiet, or if they only get more upset, you may need to reevaluate your approach. Each child is an individual, and what works for one might not work for another. Rather than continuing to use a tactic that isn't working, be open to switching gears and looking for more creative solutions. For example, if they seem bored, try teaching through games and fun activities. If they are too angry to use their words, you can ask them to write their feelings down or draw a picture.

In all difficult interactions, you should remind your child that you're empathetic to their concerns and that you care about them. Sometimes we do things that upset our kids, like requiring they complete their chores before they can go outside and play. You should remain firm with these rules, but also ensure your child feels like their emotions are being validated and not dismissed. If they get angry about their chores, you could say, "I know they're not as fun as playtime, and I see that you're upset, but it really helps me when you clean up after yourself. Can you help out even though you want to play more? Maybe we can turn clean-up into a game too."

As kids get older, it's a good idea to give them some agency and let them flex their problem-solving muscles. Instead of deciding on a solution to the conflict yourself and telling them what to do, allow them to decide. For example, if your child is upset and having trouble calming down, you might ask them, "What kind of activity would you like to do to relax?" and let them choose if they want to color, read, cuddle with you, or spend some time alone in their room depending on what they feel they need. This way, you are both working through the experience, and you show your child you trust them to figure out their own emotional needs with your help.

Here are a few more basic tasks you can do at home to support the development of emotional intelligence:

- **Show empathy**: Work to understand why your child feels the way they do and demonstrate that you care about their opinions.

- **Be a model for appropriate expression of emotions**: Set a good example for your child. Be honest with your own emotions, and manage them appropriately without letting them overtake you.

- **Teach healthy coping skills**: Give your child plenty of options for how to express themselves and calm themselves down that don't cause harm to themselves or others.

- **Turn emotional intelligence into an ongoing goal**: There is no threshold at which you can stop learning more about emotional intelligence. Take active steps to teach it, and always be open to expanding your child's knowledge and helping them practice their emotional intelligence skills.

- **Discuss challenges**: If your child is going through a difficult life situation or you notice they're having trouble with a certain emotion, set time aside to talk to them and come up with a solution together.

- **Work on your strategies for coping with emotions**: Evaluate the effectiveness of your coaching strategies and make adjustments when it seems like your child isn't getting the full benefit out of your lessons. Ask them if they think you could improve your approach in some way, and keep an eye out for times when you might slip back into dismissal or disapproval.

- **Help others**: Teach your child to be a positive force in their friend group and community by helping others, whether you volunteer for an organization or lend the neighbors a helping hand. Comfort others when they need support, and your child will learn to follow in your footsteps.

These are just a few of the many different ways you can encourage emotional growth. As you practice being an emotion coach for your child, you'll get a feeling for what works, what doesn't, and how you can adjust your methods to help your child succeed.

Games for Encouraging Emotional Intelligence

In addition to the exercises mentioned above, you can also use games to teach your child about emotional intelligence. Kids learn a lot while they're playing; this is why games have become so prevalent in the classroom. When kids are having fun, they're more receptive to new information, and their minds and bodies are engaged. They'll internalize lessons without even knowing it, which means practicing emotional intelligence will come naturally to them in real-life situations.

Conversational EQ Game

The Conversational EQ Card Game is best suited for kids five or older. It is a special deck of cards decorated with different emotional discussion prompts and point values on the back. Players take turns drawing cards and performing the task on each one. Cards may have emotions and directions such as "I feel," I think," "ask permission," and "open question." The "I feel" and "I think" cards direct players to make an "I statement" about the emotion on the card. They might say, "I feel happy when mommy plays games with me," or, "I think meeting someone new can be scary." For the "ask permission" cards, the player should ask if it's okay for them to share their feelings, before saying an "I think" statement. For the "open question" cards, a player starts with an "I feel" sentence. Another player gets to ask them an open-ended question about that emotion, to which they must respond with an "I think" sentence.

The goal of the game is to get kids to practice putting their feelings into words. The "ask permission" cards teach them about when it is appropriate to have emotional conversations, and the "open discussion" cards get them into the habit of talking about their feelings with others.

Simon Says

Simon Says is a great game for building communication skills, as mentioned in *SHHHH...Listen!*. It is equally useful for emotional intelligence, as kids learn how to listen to others with an emotional twist. In Simon Says, one player is designated as "Simon," and they give commands to the other players. If they say "Simon says" before the instruction, the players should follow their directions. If they don't say

"Simon says," they should do nothing. This is a great way to practice listening skills alongside emotional development.

To make Simon Says into a great emotional intelligence game, choose prompts that encourage kids to display different emotions. You might say, "Simon says make an angry face," "Simon says smile like you're really happy," or, "Simon says stand like you're confident." As kids get older, you can introduce more complicated emotions or ask kids to react like they would in different situations.

Self-Esteem Jenga

Helping your child build their self-esteem can assist them in having a healthier relationship with their emotions in turn. Kids who are self-confident are less guilty and fearful in regard to their emotions, and they have little trouble expressing themselves. They are emotionally honest, and they are often more likely to help others in need of assistance. Self-Esteem Jenga can teach kids confidence skills that form the backbone of their emotional intelligence.

Self-Esteem Jenga is similar to the usual game, where the tiles are built into a stack and players remove one tile at a time to keep the tower from toppling over. However, there is an added step of writing different prompts, tasks, and questions on the tiles before you build the tower. Each time someone removes a tile, they must complete the task written on it. Some ideas for prompts include talking about something that makes them happy, asking when the last time they got upset was, asking what skills they excel at, or having them come up with something their friends like about them. These boosts in self-confidence help kids see how their actions impact others and reduce feelings of shame and embarrassment.

Stop, Relax, and Think

Stop, Relax, and Think is a board game that helps kids make decisions about how they want to react when they feel various emotions. It can assist them in curbing impulsive behaviors, reminding them to calm down and think before they react. The game includes dice to roll as they move across a board, progressing through the four zones "feelings," "stop," "relax," and "think." They draw cards and collect points for completing various activities like answering questions about their emotions and listening to when others ask them to stop a certain behavior, which can help them practice the same behaviors when they face emotional turmoil in the real world.

The Fox and the Rabbit

The Fox and the Rabbit is a group game that is good for teaching self-management skills. The only supplies you need are two balls of different sizes or colors. One ball is designated as the "fox," while the other becomes the "rabbit." Have everyone stand in a circle and give each ball to kids on opposite sides of the circle. Kids can only hold either ball for a few seconds, and they shouldn't wait too long. The rabbit ball is trying to escape the fox, while the fox is trying to catch up to the rabbit. Kids must pass their ball in a way that helps it achieve its goal, based on where the other ball is.

This game is primarily about helping kids make decisions and take responsibility for their choices. Passing the ball the wrong way could result in the fox catching the rabbit, or widening the gap between the two. It also encourages kids to pay attention to what others are doing when they make their own choices, then react accordingly.

Which Emotion am I?

In this game, kids each get a card with the name of an emotion on it. They attach the card to their forehead with a rubber band or other headband without looking at it. The other kids must then help them guess which emotion is on their card by making the corresponding facial expression. If someone's card says "anger," the other kids might frown and puff out their cheeks. This teaches all players to model emotions and also to recognize others' emotional displays.

The Social and Emotional Competence Game

This is another board game tailor-made for teaching emotional intelligence. The board is divided into five sections, which are "communication," "caring," cooperating," "getting along," and "sharing feelings." Kids are encouraged to practice various skills related to each section, which helps them learn how to form and maintain healthy relationships with their peers and adults. Questions include conflict management, showing compassion, and team-building exercises.

Playing any of these games with your kids gives them a safe way to practice different emotional skills. You can also come up with fun games of your own that teach similar lessons, so long as they help you start a conversation about feelings with your child.

Chapter 3

Integrating Emotional Intelligence into Everyday Learning

Parents play a large part in teaching kids about emotional intelligence, but this education doesn't just happen inside the home. It's also part of the education kids receive at school, whether inside the classroom or out on the playground. As kids start attending school, they might make their first friends outside their family, and their social circles will start to grow. They'll also probably experience their first arguments with people their own age, and learn how to apologize and compromise to help everyone get what they want.

Since kids learn so much about social interactions naturally at school, many teachers have started adopting lessons geared toward teaching emotional intelligence. This can reduce conflicts in the classroom and help kids manage their emotions so they can remain focused and motivated on their schoolwork. Many educators who view emotional intelligence as an important skill and know that it may even outrank the impact of IQ have started to use emotion-based lesson plans to provide kids with the skills they need to succeed throughout their lives. As our understanding of the importance of EQ deepens, emotional intelligence lessons become more and more prominent in the classroom.

Parents and guardians can also benefit from learning more about emotional intelligence curriculum in schools. This information can show you what to look for when selecting a school district for your child, and also enable you to talk with your child's teachers about their development and the types of teaching strategies they're using in the classroom. Even if you're not an educator, you should still learn about these new teaching styles, as you'll be better equipped to ensure your child is getting the best possible education.

Why Emotions Matter in Education

Teachers are important authority figures in kids' lives. Many of their earliest memories take place at school, and because teachers are responsible for their education, many kids come to see their kindergarten and early elementary school teachers as a source of guidance. Because of this, educators have a unique position from which they can help kids learn emotional intelligence. More and more schools are adopting techniques for increasing EQ in the younger grade levels, and for good reason. If the goal of education is to prepare kids with the skills they'll need to achieve success, then no lesson can be more important than emotional intelligence. On top of that, improvements in emotional intelligence can translate into cognitive intelligence, better grades, and greater motivation and focus.

How Emotions Can Impact Academic Success

Kids' emotional experiences have a significant impact on their academic careers. As previously mentioned, their level of mastery over their emotions can affect how motivated they are to work on classroom assignments and homework. If a child is struggling to deal with their emotions, they'll often find themselves too distracted to pay attention in class, and they may have trouble maintaining their focus on their assignments. A child who lacks emotional intelligence coaching may have a difficult time internalizing information as well because they aren't fully engaged in the lesson. Issues with attention and focus can make it much harder for a child to do well in school, so they should be addressed in all classrooms.

Part of this process involves cultivating a positive environment for learning. It's difficult for kids to learn when they feel stressed and uncomfortable, and it can be just as hard if they're going through a rough time in their lives and they try to suppress these emotions. Teachers can implement an exercise for emotional honesty such as using a classroom mood meter, which allows kids to point to different moods to describe how they're feeling in regard to their level of energy and how positive or negative they feel. This helps them see when mismanaged negative emotions might be holding a child back. Instead of proceeding with class as usual, "Taking time to recognize feelings, elaborate on their causes, and jointly brainstorm potential strategies to shift or maintain them helps ensure that adults and children use emotions effectively to create a climate supportive of learning" (Tominey, O'Bryon, Rivers, & Shapses, 2017, para. 7). When every child in a classroom is at a comfortable energy level and there are no significant emotions pulling them away from their studies, they are ready to learn.

Different emotional states can have an impact on a child's performance in school. Kids who are enjoying their studies and are hopeful about their ability to improve their grades are more likely to work hard, as are kids who are encouraged to take pride in their work. Kids may be held back by persistent feelings of anger, worry, self-doubt, and boredom, disengaging from the lesson. It's important that the classroom atmosphere encourages kids to enjoy their time spent at school. Any emotions that prevent them from doing so should be discussed and resolved so kids get the most out of each day.

Academic anxieties can also distract and discourage kids from doing their best. Some kids may struggle with a certain subject, such as reading or math. If they don't get the adequate extra support they need to catch up with the rest of the class, they can start to feel discouraged, which only makes it harder for them to pay attention and follow along with each lesson. This can, in turn, impact their performance on tests, the way they approach questions on exams and homework, and the subject they choose to major in or pursue for their career. However, these anxieties can be eased through emotional intelligence training. Some studies of child neuroscience show that "math deficits resulting from anxiety are eliminated in individuals who show activation of brain areas related to cognitive control and motivation" (Trezise, 2017, para. 2). In other words, the better a child is at handling their emotions, the easier they'll find it to let these academic anxieties go so they can focus on self-improvement.

"Emotions Don't Belong in the Classroom"

Emotions impact a child's ability to focus, engage, and retain information. By integrating emotional intelligence into the curriculum, educators can create a supportive environment that enhances both academic and personal development.

How Classroom Factors Impact Emotions

Various factors may affect how well kids are able to adapt to school and how much they gain from each lesson. Classroom factors, external factors, and individual factors all have an impact on academic success for kids.

Classroom factors are the easiest for educators to control and adjust to suit kids' needs. These include the type of environment in the classroom and the contents of the curriculum. Classroom environments that are warm, inviting, and free of tension generally have a positive impact on kids' abilities to learn. It's a good idea for teachers to encourage questions, even if they may seem silly or simple, as this allows kids to ask for clarification without any fear of being teased. Teachers should also make emotional expression a part of the class through various discussions and projects, as this provides a healthy outlet for kids who may have a difficult time at home.

External factors may help or impede a child's ability to succeed academically as well. They include things like home life and different social interactions. A bad argument at recess can bother a child while they're trying to focus on their studies, as can an argument they had with their parent or guardian. A tough event like the death of a loved one or the divorce of their parents could also make it hard to concentrate if kids don't know how to properly deal with these feelings. While teachers can't control the home lives of the kids in their classes, they can provide a helping hand where it is appropriate, listening to kids' concerns and pointing them toward healthy outlets for their emotions.

Finally, there are individual factors to consider for each child. No two kids are exactly alike, and they may have different educational needs. Some kids may benefit from hands-on learning, while others may prefer a more traditional classroom approach. Some will be shy and withdrawn, while others will be so outgoing they may try to chatter with friends through their classes. In addition to general disposition, there may be genetic factors impacting their social skills or cognitive abilities that vary from child to child. Adjusting for these factors can be tough, as there's no "one size fits all" approach. Spending time connecting with each child as an individual, imparting emotional intelligence skills to help them communicate their preferences and what they're comfortable with, can help teachers find the right way to support each child in their class.

There are multiple possible models educators can use to bring emotional intelligence lessons into the classroom. Each represents a different approach to instructing various social and emotional skills, with some focusing more heavily on the lesson plans themselves and others aiming to create a classroom environment conducive to learning these principles. Some notable models include Maslow's hierarchy of needs, social-emotional learning, and the Ruler approach.

Maslow's Hierarchy of Needs and Education

Maslow's hierarchy of needs is a theory from the mid-1900s that arranges humans' most basic needs as a five-tier list, with the needs of the highest significance on the bottom. Each tier must be fulfilled before the next one can be achieved. Starting from the base of the tiered pyramid that is used to depict the model, the needs are "physiological, safety, love and belonging, esteem, and self-actualization" (McLeod, 2020, para. 2). Physiological needs are needs that must be fulfilled for our physical well-being. They include water, food, sleep, and warmth, without which we would die. After that are the safety and security needs, and then the need for social connections. Esteem involves feelings of accomplishment and pride in one's work, while at the top of the pyramid, self-actualization refers to finding a sense of purpose and engaging in creative activities.

According to Maslow's theory, everyone's needs follow this hierarchy, even and especially kids. Recently, it has been applied to the classroom, to show how fulfilling some or all of these needs can help kids focus on their studies. For example, a child who is hungry, perhaps because their family might not be able to afford to send them in with a filling and nutritious meal for lunch, is likely to be distracted by their hunger and have a harder time learning. The same is true for kids who lack a close social group and may not feel their "love and belonging" needs are being met. Until all needs are fulfilled, they will find it harder to learn.

Once kids' basic needs are met, they can then start feeling motivation and curiosity about new subjects. This is yet another example of the impact emotions have on kids' abilities to pay attention and learn at school. Physical safety, emotional safety, and social acceptance are all mandatory parts of a supportive classroom environment. Kids who are shown they are respected and valued, and who have high self-esteem, will be able to progress faster emotionally and cognitively than kids who find their classroom environments to be alienating or even antagonistic to their ability to learn.

"Emotional Intelligence Is Not as Important as Academic Skills"

EQ is crucial for developing self-control, empathy, and social skills, which are essential for both academic success and personal well-being. Research shows that students with higher emotional intelligence often achieve better grades.

Benefits of Emotional Intelligence on Classroom Performance

Kids who are better versed in emotional intelligence experience a wide range of benefits in the classroom. As previously mentioned, they usually have an easier time paying attention because their emotional needs are met and they aren't bothered by unresolved, uncontrollable emotions. In addition to this, many emotionally intelligent kids are more engaged in their school lessons and more excited to learn. They tend to have more positive relationships with their peers and teachers, and they're often more compassionate and empathetic, which strengthens these social bonds.

Kids who excel at emotional intelligence also tend to excel at managing themselves, as well as relating to those around them. They usually have fewer difficulties staying motivated, even without external motivating factors like the threat of bad grades or deadlines. Their communication skills are typically better as well, as they better understand how their fellow students feel. This can help them come into themselves as capable, confident learners who aren't too embarrassed to ask for help when they need it.

All of these factors combine to yield kids who are in control of their emotions, great at maintaining social relationships, and who have few academic troubles. Kids who lack emotional intelligence skills may struggle with many of these tasks. They may feel disconnected from school, which can hurt their grades and leave them feeling isolated from their peers. The best way to ensure every child has a chance to succeed in the classroom and that they aren't a distraction for their fellow students is to support their emotional growth.

Social-Emotional Learning

Social-emotional learning (SEL) has been shown to have significant long-term positive effects on kids. It is "the process of developing the self-awareness, self-control, and interpersonal skills that are vital for school, work, and life success" (Committee for Children, n.d., para. 1). Developing these skills helps people of all ages manage everyday difficulties and challenges. With SEL, kids discover self-discipline, problem-solving, emotional management, and impulse control skills that directly impact their success academically, socially, and later, professionally.

Some schools have started to adopt a systematic approach to SEL in all subjects. This involves striving to create a caring and fair learning environment that encourages participation from everyone, as well as collaboration between students. Exercises for building social and emotional skills are infused into nearly every aspect of kids' daily lives, so they are always learning and practicing whether they are in class or at home in their communities. More than two decades of research has shown the many benefits of SEL, which include a 20% decrease in bullying, a 42% decrease in physical aggression, a 5-12% decrease in dropout rates in schools that adopted this policy, and a 13% increase in academic achievements among the student bodies of these schools (Committee for Children, n.d., para. 8). This method routinely increases academic achievement, preparedness for continuing education, and career success, while decreasing behavioral issues, teen drug use and pregnancy, and mental health problems. By making emotional intelligence a more prominent and consistent part of the curriculum, kids have fewer behavioral issues and are better able to pursue personal and academic success.

The CASEL Wheel and Competencies

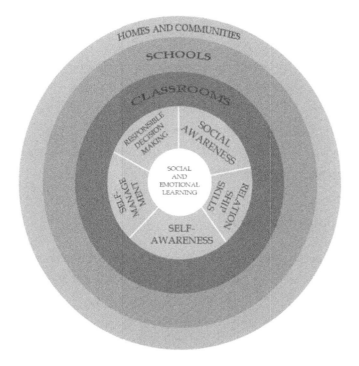

The Collaborative for Academic, Social, and Emotional Learning (CASEL) has been at the forefront of SEL for more than 20 years. In this time, they have developed a framework for SEL known as the CASEL wheel. It is based on a number of different competencies kids learn from their communities, families, schools, and classrooms. Each of these locations for learning forms an outer ring of the wheel. Starting with communities and moving inwards, the corresponding skills kids can learn are aligned learning opportunities through community programs, authentic partnerships with family members, a sense of schoolwide culture and policies, and SEL instruction in the classroom. Other key skills that make up the middle section of the wheel are self-awareness, self-management, responsible decision-making, relationship skills, and social awareness, with social and emotional learning at the core of the wheel (CASEL, n.d., para. 4).

The CASEL wheel is useful for visualizing how each aspect of a child's life affects their development. The skills toward the center of the circle are those that are most heavily enforced by educators, while the skills in the outer rings come from external sources. The wheel helps teachers identify the skills they should prioritize while still accounting for learning opportunities outside the classroom.

Approaches to SEL

SEL can vary a bit from school to school, as each educator prioritizes different learning goals. Ideally, effective approaches to SEL should include four different elements. They should be sequenced, active, focused, and explicit (CASEL, n.d., para. 3). This ideal approach is often shortened to the acronym "SAFE." Let's break each part down to better understand the important role it plays.

A sequenced approach means that the activities taught throughout each school year and between the different grade levels are coordinated in an order that makes sense. Younger kids start with easier to grasp foundation concepts and the complexity increases with time and practice. Kids don't repeat lessons for longer than it takes for them to internalize them, so they don't become bored and disengaged. They also aren't pushed to learn difficult concepts too soon, and each new idea builds off the previous one to guide kids through the lessons.

SEL should involve active lessons and nontraditional forms of learning to maintain kids' attention. Just like the games for learning emotional intelligence we discussed in the previous chapter, with more creative approaches, kids are more inclined to practice their SEL skills without feeling like they're doing work. This means they'll keep at it until they've really mastered them.

SEL teaching methods often benefit from being focused as well. It's difficult to teach many kids about emotional intelligence all at once, especially since each child may have different strengths and weaknesses. Creating a lesson plan more tailored to each child makes sure everyone is able to benefit from SEL, not just those who excel in a typical school environment.

The last important component of SEL is keeping the lessons explicit. All activities should target a specific emotional or social skill, and teachers should help kids understand how the lessons they complete translate into real-world skills with a brief recap at the end. It can help to ask kids what they feel they learned, as this makes it easier to identify if the lessons have been explicit enough.

These four components form the backbone of SEL in schools across the nation. As long as they are present, teachers may experiment with unique variations and different approaches. Some common approaches include the use of stand-alone lessons targeting a specific aspect of emotional and social competence, repeated practices such as project-based learning and cooperative assignments that build teamwork skills, and the full integration of SEL into all subjects in the curriculum. Especially dedicated schools might take this idea even further and perform a full organizational overhaul, turning SEL into a school-wide initiative to make the school's climate and culture as a whole more conducive to cognitive and emotional learning.

How SEL Skills Are Being Trained in the Classroom

SEL is a fairly recent development in most schools, so there is still plenty of ongoing training as schools begin to shift over to a more emotional intelligence-heavy curriculum. Most teachers in these schools must undergo special training before their lesson plans start to fully accommodate social and emotional skills. In schools with SEL-based curriculums, teachers are also instructed to find opportunities to reinforce these lessons throughout the day through repeated practice. For example, if students learn about sharing in the morning, they might later receive an assignment that requires them to trade supplies with other students. Kids learn a lesson, then get a chance to showcase what they've learned in a real-world scenario.

Teachers can also foster these kinds of skills in their students through their natural interactions during the school day. If a child comes up complaining that one of their playmates hurt their feelings, this can become a chance to help both kids practice their conflict resolution skills. By using a student-centered approach to instruction, teachers can have one-on-one conversations with their students and assess their emotional intelligence skills.

Some after-school programs that focus on SEL have also shown to be beneficial to kids' emotional and social skills. After-school programs naturally give kids an outlet for hyperactive emotions and a place to socialize, but they can also be of great help in reinforcing emotional intelligence lessons. These programs often reduce the frequency of problem behaviors like disrupting a lesson or getting into fights with other kids. They have the potential to greatly improve kids' self-esteem and how they view themselves, connectedness between all the school's students, grades and test scores, and positive social behaviors.

The Ruler Approach

Recognizing, Understanding, Labeling, Expressing, and Regulating emotions, also known as the RULER approach, was developed by Marc Brackett in 2005 in the Yale Center for Emotional Intelligence. It is an evidence-based method for teaching emotional intelligence that focuses on making the classroom climate as hospitable as possible. It involves integrating emotional recognition and identification into all aspects of the classroom. The approach not only improves student emotional intelligence but also often improves relationships between teachers and administrators, as well as the school at large.

Five Skills of Emotional Intelligence

The RULER approach's acronym is short for five different skills relating to emotional intelligence. Each skill is necessary for kids to learn in order to foster a positive classroom environment.

Recognizing Emotions in Oneself and Others

The recognizing part of the approach encourages kids to consider how they are feeling at any given time. Kids should ask themselves, "How do I feel right now? How can my feelings affect others?" They should also learn to identify physical signs of different emotions, such as their energy level, breathing rate, posture, and heart rate.

Understanding the Causes and Consequences of Emotions

To understand their emotions, kids should ask themselves, "Why do I feel this way? What will happen if I continue to feel this way and don't do anything about it?" They should learn how to identify different events, people, and thoughts that can affect their emotions so they can better anticipate and react to them.

Labeling Emotions With a Nuanced Vocabulary

In the labeling portion of the RULER approach, kids learn to give their feelings names. Older kids should use a more descriptive, specific vocabulary. For example, while "sad" might be a good enough descriptor for very young kids, eventually it will be more useful to use terms like "lonely," "hurt," "dejected," or "regretful" for clearer communication. This also helps kids identify the root cause of their feelings so they can come up with a specific management strategy.

Expressing Emotions in Line With Cultural Norms and Social Context

Expression of emotions must be tailored to the situation kids are currently in. If they're alone in their room, it's okay to yell into a pillow. If they're out in public, disruptive yelling or other, more aggressive reactions aren't appropriate. Kids should learn that different forms of emotional expression can help in different contexts, and they should develop a variety of different coping mechanisms they can use in each situation.

Regulating Emotions With Helpful Strategies

In the regulating portion of the RULER method, kids ask themselves, "What should I do to either maintain or ease my current feelings? What kinds of behaviors should I engage in, and which should I avoid?" Teachers can provide kids with both short-term and long-term strategies.

Some strategies kids can use to regulate their emotions include:

- Repeating an encouraging phrase or mantra to stay determined and motivated

- Practicing a breathing exercise to calm down

- Giving others the benefit of the doubt when they do or say things they don't mean

- Physically separating themselves from the source of stress

- Talking to friends, parents, or teachers for support and stress relief

Anchors of Emotional Intelligence

There are four tools that are frequently used to help convey emotional intelligence skills to kids in the RULER method. These are the Charter, the Meta Moment, the Mood Meter, and the Blueprint.

The Charter is a community-created document where everyone writes down ideas and pledges about how they intend to treat each other. It functions as a social contract that provides guidelines for acceptable behaviors in the classroom. Each child gets a say in deciding the respectful rules of the classroom that work best for everyone.

The Meta Moment is used when there are strong emotions. Kids take a step back from the situation and consider their options before impulsively reacting. They learn to choose actions that showcase their "best self," replacing harmful or ineffective reactions with more empowering ones.

The Mood Meter helps kids use more descriptive words to explain their feelings. Instead of simply saying they're "fine," kids learn to use language like "calm," "peaceful," or "excited." The Mood Meter has two axes, with one representing their energy levels and the other showing how pleasant or unpleasant their current feelings are. Once kids decide where they fall on the Mood Meter, they can then describe their feelings in more detail.

Mood Meter

The Blueprint encourages two people involved in an argument to see things from the other person's point of view. They consider how someone else might be feeling, while still acknowledging their own emotions as valid. This assists in finding a solution that works for everyone.

There are many different methods for integrating emotional intelligence into education. Whether schools stick to basic emotional education, incorporate SEL approaches, or make use of the RULER method, it's clear that emotional education has a place in the classroom and greatly benefits students.

Chapter 4

Coping With Aggressive or Defiant Kids

I t can be much harder to deal with an aggressive child than it is to manage a sad or reserved one. Oftentimes, aggressive kids may hurt you, other members of the family, their friends, or themselves. These behaviors are unacceptable in any situation. While it is fine for kids to be angry, they should never lash out and try to hurt someone, nor should they destroy property or antagonize their peers.

Aggressive behaviors aren't just harmful to others. They can also put kids at a significant social disadvantage, as they gain a reputation for being mean. Other kids might avoid them, and they may have trouble making and maintaining friendships as a result. They may have trouble learning social skills because they can't easily practice them with close friends. If you're the parent of an aggressive child, you may even find yourself feeling emotionally distanced from them despite your best efforts to love and support them.

Managing aggressive behavior usually requires formal, serious intervention. You may need to curb harmful behaviors including defiance, violence, disruptive behaviors, oppositional behaviors, temper tantrums, and meltdowns. These may occur publicly or inside the home. Either way, young kids who exhibit these aggressive tendencies need to learn alternate methods to communicate their frustrations. You can help guide them as they learn to regulate their impulses and emotional expressions by showing them what kind of behavior is expected from them and what actions are not acceptable.

Reasons for Acting Out

Dealing with an aggressive child can be exhausting at times. It is all too easy to see their behaviors as purposefully malicious and to lose your temper with them, just as they have lost their temper with you. You may even be tempted to blame the bad behavior on your child simply being a bad kid who is predisposed to violence and aggression. However, this method of thinking assumes that there is nothing you can do to limit the aggression, taking away both your agency and your child's agency. This can be very harmful, as you may start to allow these behaviors to go unchecked because you feel powerless. Alternatively, you might resort to strict punishments without trying to understand why the bad behavior is occurring. Either response only encourages kids to act out further.

The key to understanding why your child is acting out is to see it not as a purposeful, spiteful action, but instead as a bad reaction to some unmet need or other difficulty in your child's life. Aggressive behaviors may stem from all kinds of sources in kids. Just as you might be more standoffish and have a higher tendency to snap if you're feeling exhausted, stressed, or unfulfilled, so too do kids. Most aggressive kids lack the vocabulary or emotional understanding necessary to communicate their problem to you in a healthy way, so they resort to aggression. Therefore, the best way to root out aggressive behaviors is to start by figuring out why they are occurring.

Some possible sources of childhood aggression include:

- Unmet physical needs, such as hunger or exhaustion

- An upsetting situation like bullying at school, parental divorce, or the passing of a loved one

- Mental health conditions such as post-traumatic stress disorder or depression

- Learning disabilities

- Fear or anxiety about something in their lives

- A desire to impress their peers

- Overcompensating for a lack of confidence

- Seeking attention, especially if your child feels like they are often overlooked

- A lack of agency over their lives

- A failure to understand limits of acceptable behavior

- Overstimulation

- Mirroring your behaviors or the behaviors of other adults in their lives

"Aggressive Kids Are Just Bad Kids"

Aggression in kids often stems from unmet needs or emotional distress, not inherent badness. Understanding and addressing the root causes can help manage and reduce aggressive behaviors.

How to Identify the Root Cause of Anger

Many experts suggest that looking for the root cause of anger in kids provides the greatest benefits when trying to ease aggression. If you're uncertain why your child might be acting this way, look for any common factors in their aggressive outbursts. Do they tend to occur right after they come home from school, before they leave in the mornings, or only at school? Do they act more aggressively when they've spent time around certain people? Is there a specific situation that often leads your child to become aggressive? Does the behavior repeat itself around the same time of day?

Try to identify any patterns in the behavior, as this might provide more information about why they're getting aggressive. For example, if a child's aggression comes from schoolyard bullies, they might get in fights at school or be in an especially horrible mood shortly after they get home. Once you've figured out why the aggression is occurring, you can then decide whether a conversation or a punishment is necessary. You just may find that talking to your child about the difficulties they're facing may get you further than putting them in time-out or taking away a privilege each time they act out.

Bullying is a serious issue that can significantly impact your child's emotional intelligence and ability to succeed in a number of ways. If you believe your child's aggression may stem from bullying, it's important to be proactive in getting the bullying to stop. We will discuss how to identify signs your child is being bullied and steps you can take as a parent to resolve the issue in Chapter 6

"Strict Punishments Are the Best Way to Stop Aggression"

Strict punishments may escalate aggression rather than resolve it, leading to a cycle of defiance and negative self-image. Positive reinforcement and understanding the reasons behind the behavior are more effective strategies.

Tips for Maintaining a Confident, Constructive Outlook as a Parent

Even when you understand where your child's anger is coming from, it can be hard to keep a level head when you see them acting aggressively. It's natural for us to see aggressive behavior and mirror it ourselves, but this doesn't help our kids. If they yell and we start yelling right back, we've devolved the situation into a screaming match that's sure to end in tears for one or both parties. It's important to try to stay as rational and responsible as possible when your child has a tantrum or lashes out in another way. This makes it much easier to identify the cause of the anger and take steps to correct the behavior without going overboard.

If you read *SHHHH...Listen!*, you'll be familiar with this idea. If you want to help your child calm down and let go of aggressive feelings, you must first let these aggressive feelings go yourself. Only then can you effectively coach them through their emotions. Here are a few different methods and tips you can use to regain your cool when your child frustrates you.

Don't Take it Personally

If you go through life always assuming the worst from others, you may find yourself provoking negative reactions. This is also true when it comes to kids. If you anticipate your child will behave badly, or if you make judgmental and hostile decisions regarding your child's ability to control their anger, you might just end up creating the very reaction you were hoping to avoid. Nobody likes to feel like someone's just waiting for them to slip up, least of all young kids who struggle to control their angrier impulses. Avoid making negative judgments about your child before they act out or assuming their behavior is meant to purposefully aggravate you. If you're not careful, you can create a self-fulfilling prophecy.

If you find yourself feeling hurt and defensive because of your child's behaviors, take a step back and remind yourself that there's more at play here than it may seem on the surface. Avoid taking these bad behaviors as personal attacks. This helps you keep calm when tantrums occur and avoid provoking aggression in otherwise benign situations. It can also support a healthier relationship between you and your child free of mistrust and hurt feelings. Additionally, you'll avoid harming your child's long-term development by teaching them to internalize the idea that they're predisposed to being bad. By not taking things personally, you give your child the opportunity to change their behavior.

Be Realistic About Your Child's Ability to Remember Rules

We often expect kids to have the same cognitive abilities as adults, but this just isn't fair. Kids' memories are not nearly as well-developed when they are young, especially if they are struggling with emotional issues. They often get distracted, and they may break rules not out of a sense of spite, but simply because they forgot. While you should still uphold your rules, reminding yourself that genuine forgetfulness could be at play allows you to avoid enacting a punishment for a simple mistake.

Keep an eye on the pace at which your child's emotional intelligence improves, as well as which abilities they've mastered and which they've yet to get a solid grasp on. When necessary, provide calm, patient reminders, and try to remind kids of rules when they become relevant. For example, you might remind your child to share right before they start playing with a friend or sibling. This way, all the rules are laid out for your child, and they only need to follow them to meet your expectations.

Be Realistic About Your Child's Developments in Empathy and Kindness

Just as kids may take a while to fully internalize new rules or figure out how they should act in a given situation, so too do they need time to develop and utilize empathy, especially if you've just started trying to correct their aggressive behaviors. If you notice your child fails to show concern for others in some circumstances, it's likely the result of some misunderstanding rather than malice. Many kids might perceive the situation differently than how you see it, or they lack control over their impulses and act without thinking. This can lead to them causing harm without recognizing it or stopping themselves in time. Your child might also lash out because they're experiencing another source of emotional pain, just as you might snap at someone when you're having a bad day and feel overworked.

It's important to remind your child about the limits of acceptable behaviors, but keep in mind that there will be good and bad days. Your child may show great strides in empathy one day and struggle with it the next. This doesn't mean all of your efforts were for nothing; they just haven't yet had enough opportunities to practice kindness and empathy. The more experience they have dealing with conflict and practicing kindness, the better they will become at consistently being considerate of others. Some common opportunities to learn that may benefit your child include developing a safe and secure relationship with you and the rest of the family, discussing feelings and how other people hint at their emotions, being around positive emotional role models, and growing up in an environment that reinforces and provides rewards for cooperation and self-control.

Focus on Maintaining a Positive Relationship

It's sometimes more beneficial to pick and choose your battles than it is to lay out consistent punishments. Consider each situation by its own merits. Was your child being intentionally cruel or aggressive, or were there other factors at play? Would punishing your child in this instance hurt them more than it would help them? These are important questions to ask, as you never want to damage your relationship with your child if you can help it. Sometimes this means foregoing a punishment, though you should still point out when their behaviors aren't acceptable.

Many studies support the idea that positive reinforcement is better at delivering the desired outcome than punishing bad behaviors. Kids typically want to please their parents, and they'll take actions they think will make you happy. If you reward them for good behaviors, they're more likely to repeat those actions. On the other hand, strict punishments could distance you from your child as they learn to fear your reaction. They may start to act dishonestly to avoid punishment rather than actually exhibiting good behaviors for praise, which can seriously harm your attempts to guide their development.

You may find more success with the Oregon Model, which involves "weekly sessions of coaching and role-playing" that teach parents "effective ways to set limits, foster cooperation, settle arguments in a constructive way, and inject daily life with pleasant, loving activities" (Dewar, 2016, para. 47). This can help you avoid framing your parent-child relationship around negativity and the avoidance of consequences, and instead encourage you to use positive reinforcement more often.

Don't Sacrifice Your Own Psychological Well-Being

As parents, we tend to put our kids' needs ahead of our own. This can be especially frustrating when it feels like we're running ourselves ragged and all of our efforts are changing very little about our kids' behaviors. We may begin to view their actions as ungrateful, and in some cases start to resent them. This can all lead to a great deal of guilt and stress. While wanting your child to have a good life and leave their aggressive tendencies behind is a noble pursuit, it shouldn't come at the cost of your own health. The more stressed you are, the less patience you'll have for your child's outbursts, and the harder it will be to deal with them fairly.

Take breaks when you need them. Treat your well-being as just as significant of a priority as your child's well-being, and don't push yourself to the brink of exhaustion when dealing with your child. This will only put additional strain on your relationship. Care for yourself and enlist the help of others when you need to take a moment to recover. By looking after your mental and physical health, you'll be in a better position to assist your child in doing the same.

12 Evidence-Based Tips for Handling Aggression, Defiance, and Acting Out

Now that you know the importance of your mindset and some of the things you should avoid doing, you can turn your attention to things you should be doing to help your child let go of their anger. Keep in mind that while all of these tips are helpful, none of them are miraculous solutions that will yield instantaneous results. You'll need to be consistent, and you may need to repeat exercises for multiple months before you start seeing noticeable changes. However, if you stick with these strategies and you keep a level head, you're sure to see your child's behavior gradually improve over time.

Keep Kids From Overtaxing Themselves

If your child is having difficulty learning social-emotional skills, it might not be a good idea to expose them to potential sources of conflict too frequently. Your child might be able to behave themselves during the first or second interactions, but if something continues to frustrate or upset them, they may lose their temper and end up acting aggressively just because they've overtaxed themselves. It's a good idea to guide your child away from the source of their stress when you see they might be about to lash out and give them a moment to collect themselves.

For example, let's say you've noticed your child is great for the first 20 minutes of a playdate with their friend, but they start to get grouchy around the 30 minute mark. Rather than letting things progress until they lose control of their emotions, consider stepping in and cutting the playdate short. This leaves both kids seeing the interaction as a positive experience without any tears. Over time, your child's tolerance and self-control will increase, allowing them to enjoy longer playdates.

Remember the Big Picture

One of the most important things to remember is that social relationships form the bedrock of healthy interactions for your child. Kids who don't get adequately socialized are more likely to have behavioral problems because they aren't used to interacting with others. All positive relationships your child forms help them improve their emotional skills and stay connected to their friends and family members.

As a parent or guardian, you are one of the most important relationships for any child. If you're a parent, you are the first person your child ever bonded with. This is incredibly significant, as your relationship provides the blueprint for how all future relationships will go. Encourage your child to continue expanding their social circle as they grow up and meet new people, but ensure the parent-child bond remains strong at all times.

Understand Why Kids Push Back

When your child is disobedient, what is your gut reaction? There's a good chance that you assume they're being defiant on purpose. While they may know they're doing something they're not supposed to, kids rarely choose to act disobediently for no reason at all. They may be upset about something you said or did, or there may be another reason why they're reluctant to do as you ask. Pause, collect yourself, and see if you can get them to tell you why they're refusing your request rather than jumping to anger and punishment.

It's common for many kids to resist going to school when they're young. They may resist your efforts to get them ready and in the car or on the bus in the morning. Instead of getting frustrated with them, ask them why they don't want to go to school. You might find that they're experiencing a problem at school with bullies or with difficulty learning the material, or possibly just that they're anxious about being separated from you and they haven't yet made friends with their classmates. With this new information, you can alter your approach to help them feel more comfortable leaving for school, which often results in them enjoying their time at school more as well.

Reinforce Self-Control With Games

Just as you can use games to teach kids general emotional intelligence, you can also use them for reducing aggression. Using the medium of games encourages kids to listen and follow directions. It keeps a learning experience fun and makes the values instilled by these games easier to remember. Additionally, playing games with your child is a great way to spend time with them while encouraging their cognitive and emotional development.

There are many games you can play that help you impart lessons about aggression. You might choose a game that lets them work out excessive energy through harmless exercise. You can also encourage them to talk about what upsets them with the Conversational EQ Game, or roleplay different situations like dealing with bullies and having a disagreement with their friends.

Look After Yourself

Too much stress interferes with your ability to be a good teacher and parent. It's often said that you don't get a sick day when your job is being a parent, but this mentality isn't healthy. Needing a break doesn't make you a bad parent, nor does it mean you've given up on helping your child. Get some rest by doing calming activities you enjoy like reading, watching some TV, or taking a spa day while you let another family member watch your child for a brief time. Once you feel relaxed and centered, you'll be better at handling your child's aggression without getting fed up yourself.

Get Some Rest

Too little sleep makes all of us cranky and more prone to frustration. If you're tired, you're more likely to say something unkind you'll regret later. This is also true for kids, who need even more sleep than adults do. Toddlers may need as much as 12-14 hours of sleep per day to be at their best, while older kids still need around 10 hours and adults should get at least eight hours. Poor rest makes it harder to use your problem-solving skills and more likely that you and your child will resort to impulsive behaviors, which can further fracture self-control.

Foster Positive Sibling Relationships

If you have more than one child, you know how difficult it can be to dissuade sibling bickering. Sometimes your kids might get along like perfect angels, while other times they may be at each other's throats. It's important to remind all of your kids to be kind and compassionate to their siblings, even when they get frustrated with each other. Remind your kids that they're family and they need to look out for each other.

One great way to improve sibling relationships is to spend more time together as a family unit. You might have a family game night, take a weekend trip, or just make an effort to eat dinner together at the table each night. As your kids spend more time together and engage in shared interests, they'll be less likely to act aggressively toward each other and more likely to care for each other.

Defuse Negative Emotions With Reminders of Support

Kids may act out because they feel like they're alone and no one understands them. This is especially common when they start going to school, where they may feel like other kids don't like them if they're having trouble making friends. This can leave them feeling isolated and uncertain of their place in their peer group and their community.

The best way to ease this harm is to remind your child that they have people in their lives who love them and want them to succeed. Encourage them to reflect on your support and the support of the rest of the family when they need a reason to calm themselves down. As they continue practicing this method of self-soothing, they'll get into fewer conflicts and ease their aggressive tendencies, which will, in turn, help them connect with other kids and form an even larger support circle.

Help Kids Revise Their Negative Assumptions

Sometimes aggression stems from negative assumptions about how an interaction is going to go. You're probably familiar with this feeling yourself. Maybe you made plans to do something a little out of your comfort zone, and the closer it gets, the more you start regretting your decision. However, when you actually follow through on your plan, you see that you worked yourself up for no reason at all and things weren't so bad; maybe you even had fun. Kids are susceptible to making the same kinds of assumptions. They might resist spending time with other kids because they're worried about getting made fun of or being rejected, and this can make them lash out in aggression. But if you take a moment to help them see the situation as an opportunity to make new friends and encourage them to go into it with an open mind, they might find themselves pleasantly surprised.

Beware Mechanisms of Moral Disengagement

Some kids act aggressively because they don't yet have the empathy skills needed to understand how their actions hurt others, but this isn't true for all kids. Some may use aggression and fail to see how it's a bad thing because they've become convinced that what they're doing isn't bad at all. They might feel like the other person deserves their cruelty for some reason, or that it's necessary for them to achieve a certain goal. Remind your child that they're still causing harm and that everyone is deserving of basic decency from them no matter who they are.

As an example, consider a situation where your child's friend group is encouraging them to participate in the bullying of another student. Your child might know this is wrong on some level, but they also know that they need to do it to save face with their friends. However, if their friends are being bullies they're probably not good friends after all, and their actions are going to cause much more harm than good. Discuss the situation with your child and help them see that no one deserves to be bullied and they should take a stand against it, even if it creates a problem in their friend group.

Use Problem-Solving Disciplinary Tactics

Discipline is a method for correcting your child's behavior, but it can also cause unnecessary harm if you are too heavy-handed with your punishments. If your child frustrates you, you might be tempted to ground them, berate them, or even hit them. Beware punishments that do more to make you feel better than they do to help your child. Physical violence should never be part of your disciplinary method, and even groundings can be unnecessary if they don't get to the root of the problem. Instead, choose disciplinary measures that work to correct the bad behavior.

Let's say your child gets angry and shoves their plate off the table at dinner time, making a mess on the floor. You could choose to yell at them, which would leave you both frustrated and teach them very little. On the other hand, you could have them clean up the mess they made, teaching them the direct consequences of their actions and to take responsibility for the harm they cause. You could respond to a disagreement with a sibling by having them play nice with their brother or sister once they've calmed down. If your child hurts someone's feelings, just having them apologize can be enough for them to recognize how their words can help or hurt the people they care about. The punishment you dole out should be proportionate to the severity of the crime, and it should help kids recognize why their actions were wrong while giving them the opportunity to correct them.

Seek Professional Advice if Necessary

As much as we want to be the ones to help our kids, sometimes we are simply unequipped for the task. If your child has a learning disability or other special need, previously experienced trauma or is going through a traumatic experience, or if you believe there may be other unknown variables at work, there's nothing shameful about asking for the help of a professional. Child psychologists, pediatricians, and behavioral therapists can all help your child learn to express their emotions in a more positive way or provide alternate treatment methods that reduce aggression without harming your child.

Disciplining Your Child

All discipline should be carried out with the goal of encouraging good behavior and replacing bad behaviors. Discipline should never occur because it makes you feel better or functions as a way for you to vent your own frustrations on your child. This kind of maladaptive discipline usually manifests in cruel words or physical violence, which helps neither of you and does little to swap bad behaviors for good ones in the future. Instead, it can contribute to a culture of mistrust and resentment in the family, which actively stands in the way of emotional intelligence development.

Every action has consequences, whether they're good or bad. Behavioral modifications should be built off the ideal principle that good behavior results in positive consequences, and bad behavior results in negative consequences. Kids should learn and understand this rule so they can anticipate how you'll react to whatever they do. You can modify the environment around your child to facilitate good behaviors and discourage bad ones with your punishments. For example, you might send a child to their room so they can take a moment to relax and calm down in a private, safe location after getting worked up. You might need to take away TV or video game privileges if you feel like these things are contributing to bad behaviors. Making environmental adjustments can have a much more significant impact on behavior than most harsher punishments, and it rarely breeds the same kind of distrust that can strain and fracture the parent-child relationship.

Different discipline methods can be broken down into three main categories: positive punishment, negative punishment, and positive reinforcement.

Positive Punishment

Positive punishment refers to any added consequence meant to deter kids from repeating bad behavior again in the future. The added consequence should reflect the type of infraction that occurred. You might find that adding an additional responsibility to your child's list of chores is an effective way to punish positively without harming your child. For example, if you find out your child was lying about putting their toys away, a positive punishment method might be telling them they have to not only put their toys away but also straighten up their room. The added work will remind your child that there are consequences to lying. Other positive punishment ideas include having your child do something nice for someone they hurt or asking them to finish their homework as soon as they get out of school if they slack off in favor of playing games.

Negative Punishment

Negative punishments involve taking something away in response to bad behavior. This could mean physically taking something from them, like a toy or game; getting rid of privileges, such as TV time or dessert after dinner; or showing them less positive attention until they correct their behavior. You might put your child in time-out if they try to be disruptive to get your attention, or you may refuse to acknowledge a tantrum until they calm down or ask you for help calming down.

It's important to be cautious about what you choose to take away. Ideally, the item or privilege you restrict should be related to what your child did wrong, as this establishes a clear cause and effect. You should never take away something your child needs to fulfill their basic needs, like a nutritious meal or hours of sleep, as this could harm their development and make it harder for them to concentrate on being good.

Positive Reinforcement

Positive reinforcement should be used to encourage kids to repeat good behaviors. It involves giving your child something as a reward for being good. This might be something physical, like a treat or a toy, or simply giving them praise. For example, if you notice your child being kind to someone else on the playground, you might tell them what a good job they did, or offer to take them out for ice cream.

Don't forget to reward these behaviors, especially when your child does them before you have to ask. If they do their chores without needing to be reminded, this is a great opportunity to praise them. You may also allow kids to spend more time doing fun things like playing outside, watching TV, or using the computer if their behavior has been especially good.

Positive reinforcement is one of the most effective methods for teaching kids which behaviors are acceptable and which are not. Kids feel great about getting rewarded, while consequences typically make them feel bad and could harm their self-esteem. This doesn't mean you should never punish your child, but you should try to balance these punishments out with rewards so your child can see what awaits them if they can control themselves and act appropriately.

In all cases of behavioral modification, staying consistent is key. Kids need to know what the boundaries are for their behavior and what the results of their actions will be. If you are inconsistent with your punishments and praises, forgetting or purposefully not disciplining them sometimes and levying harsh punishments other times, your child will be confused, and they'll have a harder time following the rules even if they want to. Make sure your child knows what's expected of them and what will happen if they exceed or fail to meet these expectations.

Alternatives to Punishment That Support High Self-Esteem

One significant problem with using punishment to curb aggression is that it often leads to self-esteem issues. Kids begin to see themselves in a more negative light when they notice their parents are frequently angry with them. This can lead them to believe there's something wrong with them, or that they're incapable of acting appropriately, which often leads them to leave their aggression unchecked. They only become angrier with each punishment, and they may feel disconnected from you if they feel like you're being unfair.

Luckily, there are plenty of alternatives to punishment that avoid this unfortunate consequence. You can discipline your child without making them feel like they're fundamentally wrong or that they can never please you. Try these methods of discipline and watch how they allow self-esteem to flourish while still providing reasonable consequences for aggression and defiance.

Context: Tim is upset because he lost a game and, in frustration, he breaks one of his toys.

Traditional Punishment Approach:

Parent: "Tim, how many times have I told you not to break things when you're angry? This is unacceptable behavior! You're grounded for a week. Go to your room and think about what you've done."

Tim: (angrily) "It's not fair! I hate this game!"

Effect on Tim: Tim feels misunderstood and punished without being helped to understand or manage his emotions. He might internalize this as being a "bad" kid, which can negatively impact his self-esteem.

Alternative Approach:

Parent: (sees Tim breaking the toy and approaches calmly) "Tim, I can see you're really upset right now. It's okay to feel that way, but breaking your toys isn't the best solution. Can we sit down and talk about what happened?"

Tim: (crying) "I lost the game, and I got so mad! It's stupid!"

Parent: (sits down with Tim) "Losing can be really frustrating, especially when you tried so hard. It's normal to feel angry, but let's think of better ways to handle that anger. How about when you feel this way, we try taking deep breaths or punching a pillow instead of breaking things?"

Tim: (sniffles) "I just didn't know what else to do."

Parent: "I know, and that's why we're talking about it. It's important to find ways to calm down that don't involve breaking things. Let's clean up together, and later, we can think about how to fix the toy or find a way to make up for it. How does that sound?"

Tim: (nodding) "Okay, I can help clean up."

Parent: "Thanks, Tim. We all get upset sometimes, and it's good to find better ways to deal with those feelings. I'm here to help you with that."

Effect on Tim: Tim feels understood and supported, learning that it's okay to have strong emotions, but there are appropriate ways to express them. This interaction helps him learn coping strategies, feel connected to his parent, and maintain his self-esteem.

Prevention

Oftentimes the best way to discourage bad behaviors is to take proactive steps to reduce their likelihood. Many kids have difficulties with impulse control. They may have every intention of leaving the cookies on the counter untouched until after they've eaten dinner, but if they happen to walk by the package and it's within their reach, they may find themselves unable to resist.

You can help kids avoid bad behaviors by making them more difficult to engage in whenever possible. This means putting the cookies on a higher shelf or in a cabinet, where they're not so easily accessible. In other circumstances, this might mean removing your child from a stressful situation before they can get frustrated or keeping a watchful eye on them so they know you'll be there to notice any bad behaviors.

Offer Alternatives

Kids often engage in messy or otherwise unpleasant activities out of pure curiosity or a lack of forethought, often failing to notice the negative consequences of their actions until it is too late. You can offer them possible alternatives that wouldn't cause as much harm. If your child tends to break things when they're angry, provide them with a pillow to hit instead, which can withstand the beating without anyone getting hurt or anything important getting destroyed. If they make a mess in the process of learning something new, have them conduct their experiments outside, or encourage them to use something easier to clean up. These easy alternative tasks eliminate messes and stresses, redirecting attention to a harmless outlet and eliminating the need for punishment of any kind. This can also help kids feel a sense of agency too, as they can continue to do what they wanted, just in another setting or context.

Self-Reflection

Engage in self-reflection whenever possible. While the goal of this book is to help you teach your child about emotional intelligence, this involves learning some emotional intelligence skills yourself from time to time. Self-reflection can make a big difference in how you react to things your child does wrong. Ask yourself questions and check in on yourself to make sure you're not about to explode at your child. If necessary, wait to decide on an appropriate consequence until some of the anger has eased so you can be sure you're choosing something appropriate for the occasion.

Joint Time-Out

Giving kids a time-out is a common punishment. A less common version of this punishment involves giving yourself a time-out as well. This somewhat unusual disciplinary action can actually be surprisingly helpful. When your child acts out, you're likely to be frustrated as well. The time-out gives you both some time to cool off before you say or do something regrettable. It also takes both of you away from the frustrating circumstance or environment, letting you enter a neutral space together. From here, it is much easier to be kind to one another.

Use a Physical Demonstration

We often tell kids to "use your words," but sometimes words aren't as clear as more active forms of communication. If your words don't seem to be getting through to your child, try engaging them physically instead. Ask them to do something, then physically intervene and help them accomplish the task. For example, if your child starts painting and is getting dangerously close to painting on the table, you might ask them to spread out newspapers on the floor or take their supplies outside instead. Once you ask, help them follow your instructions by scooping them up and moving them, trying to make the change more fun by bouncing them or running as you do so. This turns a command into a positive exchange that's more fun for all involved.

Teach Kids to Express Remorse With Actions

Just as you saw in the previous example, actions often speak louder than words. It's one thing to ask your child to apologize after they've done something wrong. Kids may say they're sorry but still feel little remorse over their actions, only offering a half-hearted apology. It's an entirely different situation if you have them prove they're really sorry with their actions.

Observe how your child acts after they do something they shouldn't. Do they take steps to correct their behavior and make it up to you, or are they sullen and silent even after you pry an apology from them? If kids have an active role in their apologies, they'll find they can have a real impact on how well these apologies are received, and that they have an opportunity to repair the situation. Once kids know this, they're more likely to sincerely apologize and undo some of the harm they caused on their own in the future.

Practice Active Listening

Bad behavior may be a result of feeling unheard. If you have a busy household or if your other responsibilities leave you with little time to have genuine conversations with your child, they might act out to try to get your attention. While they're not getting positive attention, they may come to believe this is the only time where your whole focus is on them, which leads them to repeat it again and again. In these cases, you can reduce the likelihood of bad behaviors just by taking some time to listen to them. When your child feels like they're being heard when they're expressing themselves, they usually won't need to engage in more maladaptive behaviors any longer, as they know they have your attention without being destructive or disobedient.

Ask Mundane Questions

If you're looking for a way to help your child calm down after they've become frustrated or upset, try having them answer mundane, unrelated questions. Ask them about things that happened earlier in the day, their likes and dislikes, and similar topics. As your child answers these questions, they'll be distracted from the source of their frustration, and they'll slowly start to let some of that anger go. No longer able to fixate on why they were mad, you'll both be in a better place to assess what happened and decide what should happen next.

Provide an Expectation and Time

When we have our kids apologize or otherwise do things to make up with the person they hurt, it can sometimes come off as less than genuine. After all, we're the ones telling them to apologize, so they might not actually feel sorry for what they did at all, and they may feel like whatever we tell them to do is just another task they have to complete to avoid more punishment. As an alternative to this, let your child know you expect them to show how they're sorry, and then give them the time to do so. This way, your child can regain some of their agency and make the choice to apologize on their own. They'll feel like it was their idea all along, and they'll usually gain more from the experience since they don't think of it as something they were forced to do.

Navigating punishment and other consequences can be tricky when your child has difficulties managing their anger. You don't want to discourage them from reacting completely, but you also don't want to enable their behaviors. By remaining calm yourself, staying consistent, and seeking out methods of discipline that promote greater emotional intelligence rather than functioning purely as a reprimand, you may find that these aggressive tendencies fade away in time.

Make a Difference with Your Review

Unlock the Power of Generosity

> "Act as if what you do makes a difference. It does." - William James

People who give without expecting anything in return often live happier and longer lives. So, if we have a chance to spread some happiness and make a difference, let's grab it!

To do that, I have a small favor to ask you...

Would you help someone you've never met, even if they never knew it was you who helped?

Who is this person, you wonder? They are someone like you. Or, at least, someone who was like you once. They want to raise their child with emotional intelligence, but they're not sure where to start.

Here's where you come in. Many people decide to read a book based on its cover and its reviews. So, on behalf of a struggling parent you've never met:

Please help that parent by leaving a review for this book.

Your review costs no money and takes less than 60 seconds, but it can make a big difference. Your words might help...

...one more family have a happier home.

...one more parent feel confident about raising their child.

...one more child grow up with strong emotional skills.

To get that warm, fuzzy feeling and help someone out, all you have to do is leave a review.

Simply scan the QR code below to leave your review:

If you feel good about helping another parent, you're my kind of person. Welcome to the club. You're one of us.

Thank you from the bottom of my heart. Now, let's get back to our journey together.

• Your biggest fan, Sienna Neel

PS - Fun fact: Helping others makes us feel good too. If you know another parent who might benefit from this book, feel free to share it with them.

Chapter 5

Mindfulness for Kids: Cultivating Calm and Focus

Mindfulness has become a popular method for dealing with powerful emotions without suppressing them. It can assist in increasing emotional intelligence and improving control over how these emotions are expressed. It may help in minimizing emotional distress, easing the symptoms of depression and other mental health conditions, and dealing with general everyday stressors. While mindfulness is commonly used by adults, it shows great promise as a tool allowing kids to feel more in control of their emotions as well.

The practice of mindfulness is similar to meditation. It involves having a moment of full awareness of where we are and how we're feeling, all without judgment. Under normal circumstances, ruminating endlessly on an unpleasant emotion can leave us in an even worse mood than when we started, often because we feel guilty or ashamed about the power the emotion has over us. However, when we practice mindfulness, we can dissipate this shame and simply see ourselves in a neutral, even kind light. We accept our feelings, ensuring we don't shove them away, and we allow ourselves to feel fully so we can calm ourselves enough to decide how we can best express these feelings in a healthy way.

Benefits of Mindfulness

Kids can put mindfulness techniques to use just like adults can. It's a great practice that gives kids a totally safe way to feel more in-tune with their feelings and naturally prevents them from getting frustrated with themselves for feeling upset. It can also be used to help kids fully enjoy the experience of being happy and to assist them in recognizing the things that make them feel calm so they can use this knowledge to relax when under pressure. The benefits of mindfulness are many, and the practice should not be overlooked in any emotional intelligence toolkit.

Less Reactivity

Impulsive behaviors are hard to curb, especially if there is nothing stopping kids from leaping right to their initial reaction. If there is no reason for them to slow down and think, they'll probably jump right to getting upset, letting their emotions get the best of them. When kids routinely practice mindfulness, they get into the habit of slowing down their thoughts and processing things before leaping to conclusions. They give themselves time to consider their reaction to problems and adjust as needed, which reduces the stress of otherwise upsetting incidents.

Suppose your child is sharing their toy with their friend, and their playmate accidentally breaks it. If they're not used to using mindfulness, they might start to cry or get angry with their friend right away. They may accuse them of breaking it on purpose, even if that makes little sense. A child who is well-versed in mindfulness and emotional intelligence, on the other hand, can disregard these initial reactions and come to the conclusion that their friend wasn't trying to break the toy. This can soothe their anger and help them forgive their friend.

Improvements in Emotional Comprehension

By slowing things down, mindfulness helps kids identify how they're feeling at any given moment. If feelings pass by unnoticed, it is harder to see how they impact thoughts and behaviors. When kids pause and think about their emotions, they get more practice naming them and recognizing their effects. They can identify and acknowledge their feelings, which supports healthier coping mechanisms that aren't driven by blind instinct. Kids can also respond to stressful situations with a more open mind and a better understanding of why they feel the way they do.

Greater Emotional Recognition

Because kids learn so much about their own feelings, they also become better at spotting others' emotions. They may see watery eyes and a wobbling lip and be able to tell someone is very sad, because they've felt themselves exhibit the same behaviors when they felt the same way. They can see laughter and smiles and recognize that someone is happy because they've felt the pull of a smile on their own face and they connected the feeling with happiness. The more practice kids get identifying feelings, whether they're their own or someone else's, the easier time they'll have fitting into social situations.

Stronger Control of Emotions

The more kids engage in mindfulness, the better they become at choosing how to handle their feelings. They get used to the simple act of taking a step back and pausing before reacting. This is just enough time for them to take stock of their feelings and discard an initial reaction that seems too excessive. Kids learn to control and govern their emotional expression, and also to decide which emotions help them most for different activities. For example, feelings like positivity and excitement are more helpful at school than despair and guilt. Kids slowly learn to express the best, most appropriate emotions for their situation.

Altogether, practicing mindfulness helps kids and adults alike find their center of balance. Kids feel like they're in the "driver's seat" in regards to their feelings, controlling what they choose to express rather than being controlled by their emotions.

"Mindfulness Is Only for Adults"

Mindfulness is often seen as an adult practice, but it can be highly beneficial for children as well. Kids can learn to manage emotions, reduce stress, and enhance focus through simple mindfulness exercises tailored to their age and needs.

How Kids Utilize Mindfulness Practices

While people of all ages can use mindfulness to their advantage, it is especially useful for young kids who need some assistance with their emotions. Teaching mindfulness to kids gives them powerful, important tools they can use to navigate difficult times in their lives. They build their confidence and manage their stress levels, and they typically have more success dealing with complicated interpersonal problems.

Treat the cultivation of mindfulness like a habit. The earlier your child adopts a habit, the more likely it is to stick with them for the rest of their lives. Habits like brushing your teeth and showering are small actions we do every day to stay healthy, primarily because our parents showed us how to do them when we were small. Mindfulness is just another helpful habit to add to the pile. By teaching kids mindfulness when they're just starting to monitor their emotions, you give them a head start in emotional intelligence and provide them with a way to process their feelings they can use for many years to come. You also instill the habit of being kind, peaceful, and accepting of themselves and of others.

Since there is so much cognitive development that occurs during the early years of life, mindfulness becomes even more impactful. As kids begin to reason things out and use skills like focus and cognitive control, both of which involve the use of the prefrontal cortex just like mindfulness, they become better at patience, self-regulation, and making judgment calls. These are invaluable skills for any child.

Shaping Critical Skills

Mindfulness has the added benefit of assisting kids in developing three critical skills that are primarily developed during the early childhood years. These skills are information recall, swapping between different tasks, and having appropriate interactions with other people.

The ability to pay attention and retain information is a huge part of early education, as kids spend a large portion of their days in classrooms. Their education is equally benefited by the ability to easily switch their attention back and forth to different areas of focus, as they learn information in a number of different subjects throughout the day. Learning about appropriate behaviors with others helps them socialize effectively and maintain friendships. Other useful benefits provided by mindfulness according to various studies include increased focus, attention, self-control, participation, and compassion; improved academic performance, conflict resolution skills, and overall well-being; and decreased levels of stress, anxiety, depression, and disruptive behaviors (Mindful, n.d., para. 16). With all of these benefits, introducing your child to mindfulness is a no-brainer.

"Mindfulness Requires Long, Quiet Meditation Sessions"

Contrary to popular belief, mindfulness doesn't require long, silent meditation sessions. Simple, short exercises like mindful breathing, listening to a bell, or mindful posing can effectively help children practice mindfulness, even in noisy environments.

Basic Mindfulness Exercises

You conduct a mindfulness exercise similarly to how you would perform a meditation, with the same focus on awareness and breath. The key difference is that in mindfulness, there should be less "clearing your mind" and more consideration of your current place in the world and how you feel. It can be difficult to get kids to sit still long enough for a full mindfulness session, as they often have an abundance of energy and less patience. In this case, you can cut your mindfulness exercise down to a brief few minutes so kids can still work through each stage without giving up before they reach the end.

The three basic practices of mindfulness are mindful breathing, a body scan, and a heartbeat exercise.

Mindful Breathing

Mindful breathing involves finding somewhere comfortable to rest, relaxing your posture, and taking slow, even breaths in through the nose and out through the mouth. You can have your kids follow along with a prerecorded short mindfulness exercise, or you can guide them through it yourself. During this exercise, the goal is to help kids visualize their breath like a living thing that affects the world around them. You might have them imagine they're blowing dandelion petals away in the wind, or that they're softly blowing on a candle, light and steady enough that the flame doesn't go out. As kids keep their breaths slow and steady, their body naturally relaxes and stress melts away.

Body Scan

The body scan is one of the easiest exercises for kids to grasp. Start out by having everyone lay down on their backs and shut their eyes. Next, have them tense and relax different muscles. Start out by having them squeeze all of their muscles, then move through different parts of the body, starting with the feet and working your way up to the shoulders and neck area. This exercise is great as a way to ground kids and help them narrow their thoughts to the present moment, quieting anxieties or regrets. It also allows them to feel more connected to their bodies.

Heartbeat Exercise

In the heartbeat exercise, kids learn how their heart rate can fluctuate as they get more excited, whether this excitement comes from exercise or from their emotional reactions. They get used to noticing the feeling of their heart beating, and are subtly encouraged to consider how stress and anger might also affect the heartbeat. Begin by having kids elevate their heart rate through jogging in place or doing jumping jacks. Then direct their attention to their breath and the feeling of their heart under their fingers so they can detect the increased heart rate. You can then explain how the heart rate picks up in pace with different emotions as well.

Best Practices for Mindfulness

As in many other areas of childhood education, the best way to pass on mindfulness skills is to first learn and practice them yourself. You must embody mindfulness in order to pass it along as a good role model for your child. Let your kids see you performing a mindfulness exercise, and if they're interested, invite them to come join you. If not, let them sit quietly with you until you finish, but only if they agree not to disturb you. It's important to let kids feel like they made an active choice to participate, as otherwise, they might quickly grow bored and restless if they feel forced into it.

Try to keep the meditations simple. There are many guided mindfulness exercises available for kids online. If you'd like to use your own, you can start with a brief mantra meditation where you offer compassion and good luck to your loved ones. It may take a while for your child to settle themselves enough to complete their first mindfulness exercise, and a bit longer before you start seeing noticeable results, but in time you'll likely see them become more calm and collected in the face of emotional turmoil.

Tips for Successful Practicing

Mindfulness should be used in positive situations. It is not a punishment, though it can be a way for kids to settle themselves when they feel worried or bothered by something. Don't expect mindfulness to abruptly end bad behaviors, as it's not really equipped to do so; it is merely a way to encourage inner reflection and get kids to feel more in-tune with their feelings.

It can help to turn mindfulness into part of your daily routine. You and your child might like to do it first thing in the morning as a way to prepare yourself for the day ahead, or right after your child gets home from school to relax from the tensions of the day. It could also be a good exercise for relaxation right before bed. Whenever you decide to do it, try to keep it consistent so it becomes a habit.

You can make mindfulness even more effective by preparing a room to feel more calming and inviting. Find somewhere quiet and still where you won't be interrupted. Make sure there aren't any nearby distractions like a TV or toys. You can light some candles so long as you can place them out of kids' reach. If you practice mindfulness routinely, it may be worth setting aside a specific corner of a room as the mindfulness zone so you don't have to prepare the room each time.

Sharing your experiences is another important aspect of mindfulness. Let your child know how the mindfulness exercise makes you feel and what you gain from it. Encourage them to share their own experiences as well. If they don't seem to be getting much out of it, consider adding different exercises that might appeal to them more, and check in with them again later to see if these exercises have a more desirable effect.

Mindfulness Activities for Kids

There are many different activities you can do with kids to show them how to be more mindful. Some are more traditional meditation practices, while others are closer to fun games with an emotional spin. Here's a small selection of ideas to choose from:

Mindful Walks

Go on a walk with your child, but instead of spending the walk chatting away, turn your gaze to the scenery. Try to notice things you've never seen before, even if you've walked the same path a hundred times. Open your eyes and ears, and help your child enjoy the moment of simply existing among nature.

Listen to the Bell

This is another exercise that involves listening to sounds. You don't need to use a bell if you don't have access to one. You can substitute it for other things that make an extended ringing or chiming noise like wind chimes, dragging your finger along the rim of a glass with some water in it, or a bell sound played from your phone. Have your child close their eyes and focus on the noise, listening hard for it even as it starts to fade away. See how long the sound remains in the air and holds their focus.

Establish a Gratitude Practice

It's easy for kids to get hung up on the things they would like to have in life. Most kids look at new toys and cry if they aren't allowed to get them. Practicing gratitude is a great mindfulness exercise that can take their minds off what they don't have and help them be more thankful for what they do have.

Gratitude practice can be as simple as asking your child to identify one thing every day that they're grateful for. They might choose something they own like a stuffed animal or toy, a feeling or skill they've been working hard on, or even a friend or family member they like spending time with. This can also become a group activity for the whole family to share what they enjoy most over dinner or during a family night.

Mindful Eating

Mindful eating exercises are a staple of mindfulness education. The actions are simple. Select a small piece of food like a raisin or a square of chocolate, and leave it in your mouth. Eat it very slowly, taking a moment to recognize how it feels, how it tastes, what it smells like, and anything else you can notice. This exercise teaches kids not just to be more present in general, but also to pay more attention to their food choices. Mindful eating can help kids curb overeating as well, as it encourages them to enjoy their meals slowly.

Appreciation Practice

Appreciation practice can help kids cope with disappointment and similar emotions. When kids feel like they've been let down, it can be hard to think about all the good things in their lives. During this exercise, ask your child about what caused their disappointed feelings and why they were hurt. Then, help them shift gears. Ask them if there are other good things in their life to balance out the harm, and help them name three things they appreciate instead. This shifts their focus toward gratitude and brings them back to a calm state after getting upset while still acknowledging their feelings.

Mindful Posing

Different poses can cause us to feel differently. The most popular version of this is the "power pose," where striking a confident stance for a minute or more can actually positively impact your confidence levels. There are also mindfulness poses that allow kids to reap the benefits of pride and peacefulness. You can help your child get into the Superman pose, where the feet are planted shoulder-width apart and their arms reach up into the sky, or the Wonder Woman pose, which involves a wider stance and hands on hips.

Spidey-Senses

If your child is a big fan of superheroes, this is the perfect way to frame a mindfulness exercise. Have your child pretend they have spidey-senses and they can notice everything in their nearby environment. Using all five of their senses, have them describe the world around them, paying attention to everything they can see, hear, smell, feel, and taste. This is a unique method for helping kids ground themselves and live in the moment.

The Mindful Jar

The mindful jar is a visualization exercise for strong emotions. Start by nearly filling a clear jar with water, then adding a tablespoon's worth of glitter glue into the jar. Seal the lid tight and give it a shake. The water should appear cloudy and hard to see through with the glitter glue. Explain to your child how the glue represents their negative thoughts, which can cloud their minds and make it hard to think clearly. Next, set the jar back down on the table and let the glue settle. This shows how once they take a step back and relax, the difficult emotions fade and no longer get in the way, so they can better solve their problems with a clear and relaxed mind.

Mindful Breath Exercises

There are many mindfulness breathing exercises in addition to the basic version with steady, measured breaths. A fun one for kids is belly breathing, where kids watch their bellies rise and fall with their breaths. This can help them feel more connected to their bodies as they regulate their breathing speed. A variation on this is teddy bear breathing, where kids repeat the process but this time, they lay down on their backs and rest a stuffed animal on their stomachs. As their belly expands and contracts, the stuffed animal moves up and down along with it.

Apps and Videos

You can use technology to assist in mindful meditation practices. Many apps have video or audio recordings for your child to follow along with. Smiling Minds is a free app that hosts hundreds of meditation guides. It also has instructions for the body scan exercise. Another popular app for kids' meditations is Still Quiet Place, which has animated videos specifically catered toward young kids to keep them engaged.

Exercises for Very Young Kids

Very young kids in preschool and kindergarten may face greater difficulties trying to pay attention for a whole mindfulness exercise. To combat this, you can use very simple, brief exercises to give kids a taste of what mindfulness feels like and expand upon this later.

Try having kids simply notice their breathing and get a feel for what it feels like when they're paying attention. You can also try the five-finger starfish meditation, which involves kids holding out a hand with fingers splayed. As they breathe, have them trace up and down each finger, going up one side on the intake and down the other on the expelled breath. Especially young kids might find it easier to simply count to ten breaths, holding up a finger each time they complete a cycle.

How to Be a Mindful Family

Mindfulness isn't just about doing a certain exercise every once in a while. It becomes a part of your family. To be a mindful family is to treat emotions with respect and value, and to make sure every member of the family is comfortable talking about their feelings. It is also to express emotions in safe, healthy ways, and to take a moment to calm down before letting your emotions take control.

Mindful families follow common procedures that fall in line with their values. To become a mindful family, practice the art of embracing imperfection and forgiving people for their momentary mistakes. Listen fully when other family members are talking about their problems, and talk about your emotions without fear of judgment. Appreciation and gratitude should be core components in the household, as should generosity and support. Finally, incorporate play and having fun in daily activities. Mindful families uphold the values of mindfulness, and in doing so, improve the emotional intelligence of the entire household.

Chapter 6

Helping Kids Thrive in Tough Times

From time to time, you will have to have difficult conversations with your child. You may need to explain troubles like bullies, death, and even the dangers that linger in the world. These are tough conversations, but they can be made better by practicing emotional honesty. As hard as this may be, helping your child through the emotions that come with these circumstances is part of caring for your child.

Encouraging Your Child to Open Up to You

When you have to broach a difficult subject with your child, pay attention to possible conversation starters. Look for natural ways to ease into these discussions so kids don't feel like they're being put on the spot. You can help your child relax by starting off with non-judgmental questions that still require serious answers. You might ask them if their friends at school ever mention relationships if you want to talk about boyfriends and girlfriends with them, or who they sat with at lunch today if you suspect there might be a problem within their friend group. These questions will get far more useful answers than general questions like, "How was school?"

Give your child space to talk about their experiences and problems, and don't immediately offer advice or possible solutions. Like adults, kids sometimes just need someone to offer their sympathies, and listening can often help you learn much more about a problem than you'd get trying to solve it right away. Be sure to strike up these kinds of conversations each day, so more serious topics won't be such a significant departure from what they're used to. If you find your child isn't giving you the answers you expected or they seem reluctant to talk, take a step back and revise your approach until they're more at ease with your questions. Avoid getting angry, even if you get a rude or blank rebuff.

Be sure to remain physically engaged and emotionally available throughout the conversation. Let your expressions and gestures do some of the talking for you to avoid interrupting. Above all else, let your child know you're listening to them, and help them work through their emotions as needed.

Preschoolers

Because of their age, you should ask preschoolers more direct, specific questions to encourage them to open up about a subject. Instead of asking about the best part of their day, ask what part of their lunch they liked best, or ask them to choose between two options so they can easily assess their emotions and come to a solution.

If you notice something is off from your observations, ask them about it in a gentle, open way. You might mention how they had a certain expression when you picked them up after school and ask why. If they tell you something happened that made them upset, avoid overreacting. It doesn't help your child to immediately involve you in their affairs if they'd rather handle things on their own. Make sure they're not being harmed, empathize with them and offer your help if needed, and allow the conversation to move on when your child is ready.

Little Kids

Little kids are more comfortable with moments of silence. You may feel closer to your child when you simply spend time together, whether you're speaking or not. This can be a good exercise at the end of the day when you're both letting the stresses of work and school slide off your backs. Moments like bedtime tuck-ins and car rides are great opportunities for low-pressure chats. It's also a good idea to make sure your day includes some parent-child bonding time. You might sit down together to play a game, work on a puzzle, or help them with homework, but whatever you choose make sure you are strengthening your bond by spending time together.

Big Kids

Once again, car rides provide an excellent opportunity for a conversation with low stakes. Take advantage of this time and other moments of stillness to talk, and remain neutral when your child opens up to you, only interjecting if they ask for a response. Otherwise, allow them to vent some of their frustrations and largely work out a solution to their issues by themselves. If you're talking face-to-face, pay attention to body language, which can often reveal more than their words. While you don't need to make a point to bond with older kids every day, it's still a good idea to schedule something at least once a month.

Handling Avoidant Behavior

You may encounter times where your child reacts strangely to your questions and you start to suspect something is wrong. One common trouble is kids clamming up instead of sharing their feelings and experiences with you. If you believe they're being quiet because they're hiding something from you, consider what might make them act avoidantly or lie. They may feel embarrassed, or they may be doing something they know they shouldn't. The best thing you can do isn't to push them until they admit what they're hiding. Instead, give them the opportunity to come talk to you when they're ready, and remind them you'll care about them no matter what they may be hiding.

If you do feel the need to confront your child, speak plainly and directly without trying to catch them in a lie. Explain that you want to know the truth because you're worried about what might actually be happening. Avoid getting angry when they finally open up, even if the truth is worse than you pictured. This only teaches your child not to be honest with you in the future and that they would have been better off keeping the secret.

If your child simply seems reluctant to talk because they're tired, let them cool down first before you ask about their day. You can tell them, "I'd love to hear what happened today whenever you're ready," so they know you're happy to wait and open to hearing about it at any time. Once they feel like talking, ask specific questions. Keep an eye out for signs that your child might want to talk to you without knowing how to bring something up, like following you around or asking to do an activity together, and make sure to give them your attention during these times.

"Children Should Be Shielded from Difficult Conversations"

Shielding children from difficult conversations, such as those about bullying or family issues, often leaves them feeling more confused and isolated. Honest, age-appropriate discussions help children understand and cope with challenging situations, fostering emotional resilience.

Communicating During Difficult Situations

There will come a point where you need to broach a truly difficult subject with your child when they begin facing adversity in their lives. Don't freak out. Help your child develop confidence by remaining calm yourself during these discussions, and let them lead the way in coming up with a solution unless they outright ask you for advice. These discussions can be a great opportunity to reinforce family and community values of support and kindness. To give your child the support they need, make sure you have a good grasp on your own feelings first. Keep an eye out for common signs of distress like a lack of interest or withdrawal, low energy, fear of certain activities, or un-usually unruly behaviors. Treat any questions with respect, and never ignore your child when they're trying to talk to you about serious matters. Let kids know they're safe with you, and remember that it's okay to honestly say you don't know how to answer a question yet and that you'll make a plan to find out. Be sure not to add more fear, and don't encourage kids to see their situation as hopeless. You can make these conversations easier by bringing these kinds of topics up regularly so you'll be more prepared when they become an issue for your child.

Dealing With Traumatic News or Events

If you need to convey traumatic news to your child or to help them come to terms with their feelings about the news, it's important to deal with your own feelings first. You can be honest about things like sadness and grief, but don't let them overtake your ability to parent. Keep an eye on their emotional state as well, and look out for nonverbal cues.

Open-ended questions and conversations can help you learn more about the current situation. Ask about how they're feeling, and try to get a sense of exactly what your child knows and understands about the situation. You can skip giving them extra details that aren't necessary for explaining the situation, as these may only confuse and further upset them. Allow yourself to be sympathetic toward any reactions they may have and don't pass judgment on their feelings. Instead, allow them to feel accepted and reassured. Don't avoid or dismiss the subject either, as this could encourage kids not to talk about their problems at all.

There are plenty of difficult or traumatic things kids can encounter during their childhoods. A death in the family, bullying, divorce, and child abuse are just a few of these problems that require more serious discussions, but if you follow this general guidance, you should be able to have an open and honest talk with your child regardless of the topic.

Handling the Death of a Loved One

If at all possible, discussions of death should begin before a loved one passes away. Introduce the topic when someone is injured or ill and prepare them for the possibility that a loved one may not be around anymore. If they are very young, you may need to explain what death means. You can help your child make hospital visits, phone calls, and cards to send to the person who is ill, but don't force them to come along if they aren't comfortable doing so.

After a death occurs, let your child know right away. Again, don't demand their presence at the funeral, but if they'd like to come, let them know what they can expect to see. Make sure your child knows they're secure and safe, even if you're upset by the loss. Be upfront and direct with your language; saying someone died is clearer and often easier for kids to process than saying they passed on or that they've "gone away." Let your child guide the conversation when they're ready, and listen to them if they have concerns. If your child was close with the person who passed away, help them engage in activities to remember them by, like looking at old photos or making a symbolic craft together.

It's possible that your child may worry that you will die too now that they have been introduced to the idea. If this is a concern for them, reassure them by saying something like, "I don't plan on leaving you anytime soon." At the same time, you should also provide reassurance about what would happen to them if you did die, reminding them that other family members would take care of them and help them feel safe again.

Bullying

Keep an eye out for common signs that your child may be the victim of bullying. They may lose their enthusiasm for school, to the point of developing anxiety about going in the morning. They may be less likely to talk about fun experiences with friends, and they may complain of a stomach ache from their worries. Try to involve yourself in your child's social life through conversations, just so you know who they're spending time with and who they aren't getting along with.

If your child is at a loss about what to do, creating a toolkit for them can provide them with ideas for handling the bully. Here are a few possibilities:

- Help kids come up with phrases to use as firm but non-aggressive responses to the bully, such as, "I didn't like that," and, "leave me alone."

- Engage in role playing scenarios where you pretend to be the bully and you coach your child through their responses.

- Maintain communication with your child about the issue.

- Teach your child how to use confident body language and poses to their advantage.

- Build your child's confidence through extra-curricular activities and family bonding moments so the bullying is less likely to harm their self-esteem.

- Tell your child you're proud of them for standing up to their bullies no matter what method they choose. Let them know you have their back.

"Discussing Bullying Will Make the Problem Worse"

Discussing bullying with your child does not exacerbate the problem; instead, it empowers them with strategies to cope and seek help. It openly helps children understand that they are not alone and encourages them to stand up for themselves and others.

Teach Kids the Right Ways to React

Certain behaviors can actually encourage bullying to continue, while others are effective methods for standing up to bullies. Ensure your child knows a bully can never make them feel bad if they don't allow them to affect their confidence. Encourage your child to tell the bully how they feel and ask them to stop without aggression, as this can lead to a physical fight. Have them avoid rewarding the bully's efforts with tears or other emotional blow-ups, but don't let them go into school every day accepting that they're going to be mistreated. Help your child trust in their instincts and take the path that feels right for them, and take actions of your own to help the situation.

Take Action as a Parent

As a parent, you won't be able to directly stop the bullying unless it happens in front of you. Still, you have more power over the situation by virtue of being an adult. With your child's permission, you can step in and provide support by alerting the teacher and school to the bullying problem, involving the bully's parents, teaching your child good coping skills for getting their emotions in check when they're being antagonized, and encouraging your child to stand up for other kids they see getting bullied.

Divorce

Some parents try to wait as long as possible before letting their kids know they're getting a divorce, but this only increases the chances they'll hear it from someone else first. Talk about it with them as soon as possible, and ideally together with their other parent so you can reassure them you'll both remain in their lives. Try to choose a day with plenty of free time, like a weekend, so your child can process their feelings without any rush. Regardless of the real details, try to use a narrative free from explicit blame, as getting angry at your ex-spouse may only upset your child. Still, it's important to give them a general idea of why you two are separating. You can say something like, "We're just not in love anymore, but we both still love you very much." This comforts them while still being as honest as possible without causing distress.

Let your child know what kinds of changes they can expect and what will stay the same. If one of you is leaving the house, let them know before it happens. Let them ask any questions they need to, and allow them time to react in whatever way they see fit without taking it personally. Some kids may be hurt, and some may believe it's their own fault. Work to consistently reassure them that they did not cause the divorce and they shouldn't blame themselves. Let them adjust to the news before you start to settle into old routines again, as they may become more upset if you try to carry on like nothing is happening. Emotional honesty and openness is key.

Child Abuse

Each situation of child abuse is different, and it should be handled with care. Some kids may appreciate keeping routines as normal as possible while still working to protect them, while others may have trouble going near areas they associate with their abuse. If necessary and if your child is comfortable with it, speak to a child therapist or involve the authorities, but let your child make the decision. Helping them feel a sense of agency is incredibly important.

It can be hard to find the right words to talk about this topic with your child. If you suspect your child might be the victim of abuse, avoid being accusatory, and don't make promises you cannot keep. For example, don't tell your child you promise not to tell anyone, as you may need to in order to guarantee their safety. Instead, tell them you promise to do what you can to help them, and that you won't tell anyone who doesn't need to know. Instead of asking directly if someone touched them inappropriately, you can ask if there's something bothering them and allow them to lead the conversation.

Your child may have questions of their own when discussing the topic of abuse or talking about their experiences. Here are some common questions and possible answers:

- **What is child abuse?**: Child abuse involves an adult purposefully hurting a child. It can be physical, emotional, neglectful, or sexual.

- **Is it my fault if it happens to me?**: Child abuse is never the child's fault. Reassure the child that it is always the fault of the adult, no matter what actions they may have taken.

- **How can I make it stop?**: Many child abusers tell kids they'll be in trouble if they tell someone what's happening, but this is just a way to threaten them. The best way for a child to escape an abusive situation is to tell a trusted adult and allow them to help.

Chapter 7

Building Resilience: Strengthening Your Child's Inner Fortitude

It may be hard to picture if your child is still young, but there will come a time in their lives where you are no longer constantly around to help them, and they will need to start handling their emotions on their own. They may start to draw away from you and establish their independence as they become teenagers, or this distance may only start to appear when they move away to college or move out of the house as an adult. At a certain point, all kids learn to lead their own lives. There will be times even while they are young, such as when they are at school or a club meeting, that you won't be around to protect them either, and they will need to learn emotional resilience to deal with difficulties and stress from different sources in their lives.

Your ultimate goal as an emotional intelligence educator is to help kids cultivate their emotional skills so they can cope with their feelings by themselves. Emotional resilience represents their ability to handle the different ups and downs they'll experience in their lives, as well as moments of great change. Resilience helps kids find their footing in unfamiliar circumstances and allows them to withstand more significant shake-ups like the end of a relationship, moving, or experiencing grief. It becomes a large part of mental health management as kids get older and enter adulthood. It's important for kids to start building resilience as soon as possible so they can withstand these tough times and much more.

"Resilience Means Never Feeling Hurt or Sad"

Resilience is not about avoiding or suppressing negative emotions; rather, it involves recognizing and managing these feelings constructively. It helps children cope with adversity, recover from setbacks, and adapt to challenging situations, fostering emotional strength.

There will be obstacles and setbacks in your child's life, no matter how much you may want to prevent these as a parent. While you can't clear your child's path entirely, you can give them the tools necessary for them to overcome these difficulties so they can avoid stress and anxiety. In fact, dealing with these setbacks can help kids gain experience with emotional intelligence if they have a difficult time learning in more traditional ways. They may strengthen their self-awareness and self-advocacy abilities, boost their self-esteem, and expose them to different strategies for emotional regulation and self-improvement.

In this way, while these obstacles aren't necessarily a good thing, they help to build character and support healthy development.

How to Help Your Child Cultivate Resilience

Resilience is a skill that can come from many different sources. It can be a natural product of experiencing a difficult moment in life and making it through to the other side. Kids can develop resilience by relying on support from their families, friends, and community members, as they never truly face adversity alone. And of course, parents play a major role in helping their kids develop resilience. Each of these methods can be useful and impart different lessons to your child.

Parents and Other Adults

It's very likely that you've experienced some form of hardship during your life. Maybe you struggled to fit in as a child. Perhaps you had some financial troubles that made you worry about your ability to afford everything you needed to live safely and happily. You may have experienced a significant loss and the grief that comes along with it. Whatever your life experiences, you know what it is to experience pain and hurt, and to make it through this hurt to reach a supportive, loving environment once again. Therefore, you are the best possible role model for resilience for your child. You are living proof that the difficulties you face do not have to define you. When your child sees how calm and collected you are in the face of things that frighten them, they'll become a little braver in turn.

You can also support resilience by teaching your child necessary problem-solving skills. Kids who learn to tackle problems, first with your support and then on their own, are better at recovering from unfortunate events. They are often able to find a suitable solution for their problems, and if not, they are strong enough to hold out until the rough seas of life have calmed down, all because they learned their resilience from you.

Social Support

Kids have an easier time exhibiting resilient behaviors when they know they have a loving, dedicated social circle to back them up. Kids need to feel supported, as do adults. Without social support, it would be very difficult for kids to tackle problems head-on or take risks. With the encouragement and backing of their families, their communities, and their friends, they are emboldened to take on even the toughest of tasks.

"Shielding Children from Stress Helps Build Resilience"

Shielding children from all stressors can actually hinder their development of resilience. Experiencing manageable levels of stress, with guidance and support, helps children build coping mechanisms and learn to navigate life's challenges effectively.

Moderately Stressful Situations

A small amount of stress may be difficult in the moment, but it helps kids get a sense of the difficult moments that may await them later in life. Therefore, some stress can be good, so long as it does not become overwhelming. Kids will be expected to push themselves a little harder, and they may find that their limits are much further than they expected them to be. These semi-stressful situations set kids up with skills they'll continue to rely on for much of their lives.

Practical, Powerful Strategies for Building Resilience in Kids

Kids can benefit greatly from getting some resilience practice in. A small stressful situation may help them feel a little more comfortable with the idea of testing their limits, but they may face much more significant disappointments in their lives. Because of this, it's important to take every possible opportunity to educate kids on resilience so they'll have it when they need it most.

Help Kids Build Social Connections

There is very little that's more comforting for kids than having a good support group. Always work to increase the amount of time your child spends around people who support them. It's very likely that at some point, they will come across people who don't want to see them succeed. You can counteract this by repeatedly and frequently showing your child that there will always be people who are supportive of their dreams and goals. Let them know it's always okay to ask for help when they need it. This knowledge will provide them with strength in their most hopeless times.

Support Their Executive Functioning Skills

Executive functioning involves important skills including self-control, critical thinking, and working memory. These kinds of skills are significantly helpful for resilience, as they are all part of problem-solving and emotional management. Some behaviors involved in executive functioning include healthy social behavior, as modeled by you; establishing consistent routines; creating and maintaining supportive relationships; providing opportunities for social connections completely unique to your child, such as friendships outside the family and romantic relationships; games that involve memory and engage kids' creative thinking skills; and chances to think and act independently based on your child's own decisions. You can practice each of these behaviors with your child on a regular basis.

Incorporate Exercise

Many people use exercise as a way to channel their emotions into positive energy. Some have used it as a method for expressing their grief in a constructive way, while others have used workouts to cope with a serious life event like a new job or a breakup. Staying active helps kids remain healthy, and it serves as a great outlet for lots of pent up energy your child may be carrying around. On top of that, it's an excellent healthy habit for adults to practice, and the best way to convince yourself to exercise later in life is to practice it religiously as a child.

Nurture Feelings of Competency and Optimism

When we get discouraged or disappointed, we tend to forget just how much we are truly capable of. Sometimes we need to be reminded of everything we do well. Don't forget to let your child know what they excel in and how proud you are of them trying their best, no matter how their results pan out. Praise your child for the effort they put into their tasks, and reassure them that even if it doesn't seem like they're the best suited for a task at first, they can always try to improve. With enough dedication and practice, they're sure to succeed, regardless of what they're up against.

Help Kids Reframe Challenges and Face Fears

Some challenging or frightening situations can appear scarier at first glance than they actually are. For example, your child may stress out about an upcoming math test, worried they're not going to do well and their grades will suffer. To counteract this, you can point out that this math test is just one part of a larger grade, and even if they don't do as well as they hope, there are other ways to keep their grades up. You may also remind them that grades aren't everything, but if they want some help studying, you would be happy to assist them. By providing your support and reducing the threat of the challenge, you take away some of its power and remind your child that they are capable of handling almost anything.

Let Kids See How You Handle Disappointment

Many parents are afraid to show their negative emotions around their kids. They remain somewhat distant and withdrawn, which can leave kids wondering why they never see their parents struggling the same way they do. Rather than helping your child grow, this practice only leaves them seeing themselves as lesser or deficient. It can help to let your child see how you handle a wide range of emotions, especially disappointment. Be honest with them and explain that while you're not happy with what happened, you know that there will be another opportunity for something good to happen later, and that you'll make it through this tough moment if you stick to your healthy coping strategies. By seeing that their parent is just as capable of getting disappointed as they are, but also that this feeling can be managed, your child will likely be inspired to face their own disappointments with the same level of resilience.

Encourage Relatively Safe, Considered Risks

Sometimes, it's necessary to encourage kids to take risks and see how things pan out for themselves. This doesn't mean you should let them experience a complete trial by fire, but it does mean that if you find yourself acting like a helicopter parent from time to time, you should try taking a step back and letting them make some mildly risky decisions. Experience is the best way for them to learn, after all. If they never try to take risks in their childhood, they'll have trouble taking advantage of opportunities later in life.

Let Kids Experience Consequences and Lessons

Risks may not always pan out, and bad decisions come with consequences. When this happens, it's tempting to want to sweep your child up and protect them from any possible harms that could befall them. However, this just isn't a realistic method of parenting. Sometimes, it is necessary to let your child lie in the bed they've made so they can learn from the experience. If they fail a test because they spent the night watching TV instead of studying, let them deal with the failing grade. Next time, they won't be so quick to brush off their responsibilities.

Give Kids Some Agency

This is another resilience-building strategy that encourages letting kids make their own choices. When they're very young, you can start by offering them small, less significant choices and allowing them to decide what they want. For example, you could ask them what side they want with their lunch out of three different options. As they get older, you can let them make more important choices, while still being around to offer advice and support them should they need it. Letting kids experience a little agency helps them feel more in control of their lives. It also reduces the chances of them making unsafe decisions when they move out or go to college, as it won't be the first time they've felt like they were in charge of themselves.

Nurture a Growth Mindset

Many kids feel more limited when they feel like they are only good at certain subjects. They make the mistake of believing they aren't capable of getting better at the things they don't immediately excel at, which discourages them from trying new things. This is in stark opposition to the growth mindset, which suggests that with enough practice and attention, people can learn any skill they want. A growth mindset is healthier and helps kids be more productive, as they don't box themselves into certain assumptions about who they are and what kind of person they can be. Kids with growth mindsets aren't nearly as negatively impacted by failure, as they know they can always try again and they might have more favorable results next time. This helps them remain resilient even when things aren't going their way.

Help Kids Create a Problem-Solving Toolbox

Plenty of parents try to solve their kids' problems for them. They interject themselves into every issue, often calling the school or other kids' parents, frequently getting involved without their kids asking them to. While it's good to have your child's back through thick and thin, there will come a time when they need to stand on their own two legs without backing down. If you've been intervening too frequently, your child might not have the experience they need to deal with problems by themselves.

Rather than directly interfering, try creating a problem-solving toolbox for your child. The problem-solving toolbox contains different strategies for conflict resolution, emotional control, stress management, and other necessary activities that could otherwise be hard for kids to tackle alone. Encourage your child to develop their own strategies for dealing with personal and academic issues, and they will naturally add these strategies to their toolbox for future use.

Use Delayed Gratification

Instant gratification is a deceptively dangerous habit for kids to indulge in. It represents the idea that the immediate pleasure that can be gained from an activity is more desirable than long-term results. Indulging in instant gratification means giving up a better reward for something easier. An example of instant gratification might be your child choosing not to do their homework in favor of playing with their friends. In the moment, it is much more fun to play with friends than it is to read a textbook. However, the next day when their homework is incomplete for class, they may regret giving into instant gratification.

Delayed gratification, on the other hand, encourages kids to hold out for the better long-term reward. Maintaining good grades is much more valuable than a few extra minutes at the playground, so the homework should be prioritized. This can often be difficult for kids to understand, as they are impulsive and want the easy prize without the extra work. You can help your child understand the value of delayed gratification by asking them to weigh the value of two things in their head, one a short-term pleasure and the other a long-term achievement, and think about how they'd feel if they had each one. The long-term achievement holds more weight, so kids will eventually start to see the value in holding out for the better prize. As a simple example, ask them to choose between getting one piece of candy now, or behaving themselves while you run errands and getting two pieces after. The two pieces of candy should win out, which means your child not only learns about long-term goal setting but also practices their good behavior skills.

Delayed gratification ties into self-control and self-discipline, which are key factors in remaining resilient. If kids remember that there is something better waiting for them at the end of every one of life's difficulties, they will be able to withstand these difficult situations without issue.

Avoid Sink or Swim Situations

Kids learn best when they can try out some things for themselves, but they must also know they are supported and loved. They want to branch out and explore the world, but they also want to know they have a home base to come back to. Let your child try new things and put themselves out there while reminding them you are here for them should they need it. This will provide them with the confidence they need to tackle their new passion head-on.

Your child may also benefit from learning to ask for help more fre-quently. Encourage them to talk to teachers when they don't under-stand a new concept, or to ask their fellow students for help. You can also use the scaffolding approach to providing support, which involves offering a lot of support at the beginning of the exercise and slowly walking it back, letting your child take the reins as time goes on. This is similar to how you might teach them to ride a bike, starting off with training wheels and steadying hands, and eventually letting them ride on their own.

Activities for Teaching Grit and Resilience

Resilience can also be taught through encouragement and trying out various activities. Practice them with your child to help them refine their emotional management skills. You'll also help your child develop grit, which is a mixture of passion and perseverance.

Assist Kids in Identifying Their Goals

Everyone needs something to work toward in their lives. The pursuit of goals is at the top of Maslow's hierarchy of needs. It represents a feeling of self-fulfillment we get from feeling like we've found our place in the world. You can help your child achieve this same feeling by walking them through the process of creating goals for themselves. You can assist them in creating a mood board, or even just daydreaming and journaling about their goals. Consider both short-term goals that can be accomplished now and long-term goals they can strive for their whole lives.

Encourage Your Child to Talk to People With Admirable Goals

Kids naturally look up to their parents, but there are plenty of other people who might be good role models for your child as well. Consider people you can get in contact with who have goals similar to your child's ambitions, or who have especially altruistic goals, and who work toward those goals each day. Show kids that hard work and perseverance really does pay off and that their dreams are entirely achievable if they believe in themselves and they're willing to work for them.

Use Nature and Literature

There are plenty of examples of grit and resilience to be found in the world around us. You only need to look outside to see them. Show your child how grass or flowers might push through the cracks in the sidewalks to grow in inhospitable conditions, which shows a remarkable amount of resilience, or let them watch documentaries about animals that live in harsh environments or otherwise demonstrate the value of hard work. You can also look to books for these inspirational stories. One especially well-known children's story is *The Little Engine That Could*, which is all about the power of persistence and positive thinking.

Ask Kids What the Hard Part Is

When your child seems discouraged and they're ready to give up on their task, help them find the will to keep going by asking them, "What's the hard part?" When they answer, help them break this difficult roadblock into smaller, more manageable pieces by gently guiding them toward a more incremental approach. Let your child figure this new approach out themselves so they get the experience of flexing their problem-solving skills.

As an example, let's say your child is trying to complete a drawing and they're having difficulties. When you ask what the hard part is, they say they can't get the tree to look right. They can then break the process of drawing the tree down into its smaller parts—an evergreen tree is little more than a small brown rectangle for a trunk and a big green triangle for the branches. Thinking about hard tasks in terms of their smallest, simplest components breaks down barriers to success and teaches kids to tackle other problems in much the same way.

Follow the "Hard Thing" Rule

The "hard thing" rule is a study in dedication broken into three rules. The first rule is that everyone in the family has to pick something hard to focus their efforts on for a while. Usually the time period is around a month minimum. The task should be difficult enough that it requires multiple attempts and some trial-and-error to get right. The second rule is that everyone gets to choose their own hard task. The third rule is that whatever you choose to start, you have to finish. This encourages kids to pick up new skills, try out new experiences, and broaden their horizons, all while having them stick with it long enough that they can see their hard work pay off.

Grit Pie Exercise

The "grit pie" activity is meant to help kids practice optimism. The pie is symbolic of a larger obstacle your child is facing, while each slice of the pie functions as a 'slice' of the problem. For example, the whole pie might be doing well in math class, and the slices may include problems such as the teacher moving too fast or your child failing to turn in their homework. Decide together if each part of the issue is a permanent obstacle or if it's something temporary that will go away soon. When the issue is broken down this way, your child will discover that very few issues have permanent reasons why they're problems after all, and that the vast majority of the slices are usually temporary troubles they can easily overcome. A teacher moving too fast might become more manageable with additional math tutoring, and ensuring your child finishes their homework first thing after school ensures they get the practice they need to really learn the lessons. What was once a significant issue is easily solved through divide and conquer.

Share Your Passions

Kids enjoy being able to share fun activities and quality time with their parents, and getting your child involved in your favorite hobby can be a great way to bond. Show your child how excited the hobby makes you and how it's okay to show enthusiasm for what they love. By sharing your passions, you also teach your child that they can pursue their dreams and goals, finding hobbies and even a career they love rather than settling for a job they don't particularly enjoy. This helps your child feel truly limitless.

Keeping the Game Alive

Now that you have everything you need to help your child develop emotional intelligence, it's time to share your newfound knowledge and guide other parents to the same help.

By simply leaving your honest opinion of this book on Amazon, you'll show other parents where they can find the information they're looking for, and keep the passion for raising emotionally intelligent kids alive.

Thank you for your support. Emotional intelligence in children thrives when we pass on our knowledge – and you're helping me do just that.

Simply scan the QR code below to leave your review:

Concluding Insights

A t this point, it should be incredibly clear to you just how important emotional intelligence is. EQ is a foundational skill upon which many others are built later in childhood development, including socialization, critical thinking, problem-solving, showing compassion, and much more. Kids who are adequately emotionally prepared tend to experience greater success in their personal relationships, academic careers, and later professional lives. Though the benefits of emotional intelligence remain significant throughout our whole lives, education about feelings is most effective when it starts in early childhood.

As a parent, teacher, or other guardian, you serve as your child's introduction to emotional intelligence. You are both the model upon which they will base themselves and the instruction manual for navigating their various, often confusing feelings. You also provide feedback about how well your child is managing their emotions. You can guide them toward a healthy relationship with their feelings where they appropriately express how they feel and respectfully engage with others.

It is never too early to start teaching kids about their feelings. The more fluent your child is in emotional literacy, the fewer problems they'll face because of a failure to read the room or an unintentionally upsetting behavior. They'll be able to form strong bonds with their peers with the potential to last a lifetime. Emotionally intelligent kids are typically well-liked at their workplaces, and they often have an academic advantage as well, since they are more motivated and driven. In short, there is very little a truly emotionally intelligent child cannot do because they have the self-confidence to put their best efforts into any task and the self-awareness to take care of themselves and others.

In *Raising Emotional Intelligence in Kids*, you've learned how to avoid many of the common pitfalls preventing many parents from providing their kids with adequate emotional awareness. You should now understand why proper emotional development is so critical to your child's future, as well as what steps you can take to encourage their success, whether you're helping your toddler put a name to their emotions or assisting your tween's navigation through the emotional storm that is puberty. Whatever emotional challenges come your family's way, you know you're more than prepared to face the challenge. You're ready to give your child all the tools they need to embrace the world and conquer life.

If you enjoyed this book and found it to be especially helpful, consider leaving a positive review on Amazon. This helps other parents and educators provide their kids with the benefits of emotional intelligence, breaking down barriers to socialization and creating a more compassionate and empathetic world.

References

AnnaliseArt. (2020, Mar. 24). *Exercise equipment*. Pixabay. https://pixabay.com/illustrations/workout-equipment-weights-4963665/

AnnaliseArt. (2020, Apr. 16). *Happy face emojis*. Pixabay. https://pixabay.com/illustrations/happy-faces-emoticons-smiley-emoji-5049095/

CASEL. (n.d.). *Approaches*. https://casel.org/what-is-sel-4/approaches/

CASEL. (n.d.). *What are the core competence areas and where are they promoted*? https://casel.org/sel-framework/

Committee for Children. (n.d.). *What is social-emotional learning*? https://www.cfchildren.org/what-is-social-emotional-learning/

CorrelateStudio. (2019, May 8). *Four pairs of friends*. Pixabay. https://pixabay.com/illustrations/friends-people-friendship-family-4187953/

Creozavr. (2019, Dec. 2). *Bullying*. Pixabay. https://pixabay.com/vectors/boy-girl-protection-stood-up-fight-4665536/

DavidRockDesign. (2018, Apr. 17). *Child reading*. Pixabay. https://pixabay.com/illustrations/child-i-am-a-student-book-figure-3326960/

Kadane, L. (2020, Aug. 4). *EQ vs. IQ: Why emotional intelligence will take your kid further in life*. Today's Parent. https://www.todaysparent.com/kids/kids-health/eq-vs-iq-why-emotional-intelligence-will-take-kids-farther-in-life/

Lisitsa, E. (2012, June 8). *An introduction to emotion coaching*. The Gottman Institute. https://www.gottman.com/blog/an-introduction-to-emotion-coaching/

McLeod, S. (2020, Mar. 20). *Maslow's hierarchy of needs*. Simply Psychology. https://www.simplypsychology.org/maslow.html

Mindful. (n.d.). *Mindfulness for kids*. https://www.mindful.org/mindfulness-for-kids/

Mohammad_hassan. (2020, Aug. 21). *Handing over a heart*. Pixabay. https://pixabay.com/illustrations/giving-love-apologize-kind-man-5503676/

Mohammad_hassan. (2017, Aug. 19). *Woman lifting baby into the air*. Pixabay. https://pixabay.com/illustrations/family-mother-child-adult-baby-2658143/

Morin, A. (2019, Oct. 21). *How to raise an emotionally intelligent child*. Verywell family. https://www.verywellfamily.com/tips-for-raising-an-emotionally-intelligent-child-4157946

Ohio University. (n.d.). *5 qualities of emotional intelligence*. https://onlinemasters.ohio.edu/blog/5-qualities-of-emotional-intelligence/

OpenClipart-Vectors. (2017, Jan. 31). *Superman power pose*. Pixabay. https://pixabay.com/vectors/cartoon-comic-comic-characters-2025820/

Oswalt, A. (n.d.). *Emotional and social development in early childhood*.   Gracepoint. https://www.gracepointwellness.org/474-emotional-intelligence/article/16149-emotional-and-social-development-in-early-childhood

Piyapong89. (2020, Oct. 22). *Children displaying emotions*. Pixabay. https://pixabay.com/illustrations/children-childhood-young-kids-boys-5672087

RoadLight. (2020, Oct. 9). *Rabbit and fox*. Pixabay. https://pixabay.com/illustrations/animals-cute-animals-wild-animals-5636909/

Syaibatulhamdi. (2020, Feb. 11). *Walk at sunset*. Pixabay. https://pixabay.com/illustrations/wallpaper-cartoon-landscape-people-4839630

Tominey, S., O'Bryon, E., Rivers, S. E., & Shapses, S. (2017, March). *Teaching emotional intelligence in early childhood*. NAEYC. https://www.naeyc.org/resources/pubs/yc/mar2017/teaching-emotional-intelligence

Trezise, K. (2017, July 13). *Emotions in classrooms: The need to understand how emotions affect learning and education*. NJP Science of   Learning. https://npjscilearncommunity.nature.com/posts/18507-emotions-in-classrooms-the-need-to-understand-how-emotions-affect-learning-and-education

Trotta, J. (2018, Dec. 10). *Emotional intelligence—What do the numbers mean?* LinkedIn. https://www.linkedin.com/pulse/emotional-intelligence-what-do-numbers-mean-joanne-trotta

Wixin_56k. (2019, May 7). *Bedroom at night.* Pixabay.

< a href="https://www.freepik.com/free-vector/little-son-reaching-arms-his-mom-woman-kid-walking-together-flat-illustration_11235630.htm#query=parenting&position=1&from_view=search&track=sph">Image by pch.vector</a> on Freepik

<ahref="https://www.freepik.com/free-vector/little-boy-superhero-costume_24555194.htm#query=superhero%20pose&position=49&from_view=search&track=ais">Image by brgfx</a> on Freepik

Made in the USA
Coppell, TX
21 December 2024

43231975R00090